Mussolini and Fascist Italy

IN THE SAME SERIES

General Editors: Eric J. Evans and P.D. King

LANCASTER PAMPHLETS

Mussolini and Fascist Italy

Second edition

Martin Blinkhorn

London and New York

First published in 1984 by
Methuen & Co. Ltd
Reprinted 1987

Reprinted 1989, 1990, 1991
by Routledge
11 New Fetter Lane, London EC4P 4EE
29 West 35th Street, New York, NY 10001

Second edition 1994
Reprinted 1995

© 1984, 1994 Martin Blinkhorn

Typeset in 10 on 12 point Bembo by
Ponting–Green Publishing Services, Chesham, Bucks
Printed in Great Britain by
Clays Ltd, St Ives plc

Printed on acid free paper

British Library Cataloguing in Publication Data
A catalogue record for this book is available from the British Library

Library of Congress Cataloging in Publication Data
has been applied for

ISBN 0–415–10231–6

Contents

Foreword

Lancaster Pamphlets offer concise and up-to-date accounts of major historical topics, primarily for the help of students preparing for Advanced Level examinations, though they should also be of value to those pursuing introductory courses in universities and other institutions of higher education. Without being all-embracing, their aims are to bring some of the central themes or problems confronting students and teachers into sharper focus than the textbook writer can hope to do; to provide the reader with some of the results of recent research which the textbook may not embody; and to stimulate thought about the whole interpretation of the topic under discussion.

Time chart

Before 1900

1859–70	Unification of Italy
1881	Electoral reform extends franchise to 2 million
1881–2	Italian ambitions in Egypt and Tunis thwarted
1883	Mussolini born at Predappio
1885–9	Italy occupies Eritrea and Somaliland
1892	Foundation of Italian Socialist Party (PSI)
1896	Italy defeated at Adowa
1898–1900	Period of socio-political crisis

1900–15

1902–4	Mussolini in Switzerland
1903–5	Giolitti's second administration
1904–6	Mussolini's military service
1906–9	Giolitti's third administration
1906–7	Mussolini teaching
1908	Mussolini begins journalistic career
	Revolutionary syndicalists leave PSI
1909	Mussolini in Trent
1910	Foundation of Italian Nationalist Association
1910–12	Mussolini in Forlì

1911–12	Libyan war – opposed by Mussolini
1912	Left takes over PSI
	Mussolini editor of *Avanti*
	Giolitti's electoral reform – franchise extended to almost 9 million
1913	General election – Catholic and PSI advance
1914–15	Interventionist crisis
1914	Outbreak of war (August)
	Foundation of Fasci di Azione Rivoluzionaria (October)
	Mussolini leaves *Avanti*, founds *Il Popolo d'Italia* and is expelled from PSI (November–December)
1915	Treaty of London and Italian entry into war (April–May)

1915–24

1915–17	Mussolini on war service
1917	Caporetto – Italian defeat
1918	Vittorio Veneto – Italian victory
1918–20	*Biennio rosso* – 'two red years'
1919	Fascio di Combattimento founded (March)
	D'Annunzio seizes Fiume (September)
	General Election (November) – fascist failure, PSI and Popolari become major parties
1920–2	Rise of fascism as mass movement
1920	Occupation of factories (August)
	D'Annunzio expelled from Fiume (December)
1921	General Election (May) – thirty-five fascists elected
	Abortive Pact of Pacification between fascists and socialists (summer)
	Foundation of PNF – fascism becomes a political party (November)
1922	Election of Pope Pius XI (February)
	Facta becomes prime minister (February)
	Unsuccessful socialist general strike (August)
	March on Rome – Mussolini becomes prime minister (October)
	Fascist Grand Council created (December)
1923	Nationalists join PNF (February)
	Electoral law revised

Corfu affair (September)
Chigi Palace Pact (December)
Fascist militia created (December)
1923–4   Italy obtains Fiume
1924   General Election (April) under revised system –
fascist victory
Matteotti affair (June–August) – secession of
opposition from parliament
Revolt of the consuls (December)

1923–45

1925–6   Legal and institutional basis of dictatorship created
1925   Mussolini announces dictatorship (January)
Farinacci PNF secretary (January)
Vidoni Palace pact (October)
1926   Turati replaces Farinacci as PNF secretary (April)
Rocco's labour relations law
Ministry of Corporations created
Albanian protectorate declared
1927   Labour Charter published
'Quota 90'
1928   Fascist Labour Confederation split up
Treaty of 'friendship' with Ethiopia
1929   Lateran Accords between Italy and papacy
Grandi becomes foreign secretary
1930   Giuriati replaces Turati as PNF secretary
Bottai becomes minister for corporations
1931   Starace becomes PNF secretary
1932   Mussolini resumes foreign secretaryship
1933   IRI founded
1934   Mixed corporations created
Austrian crisis – Italian troops sent to border (July)
Incident on Ethiopia–Somaliland border (December)
1935   Stresa conference (April)
Outbreak of Ethiopian war (October)
1936   End of Ethiopian war (May)
Ciano becomes foreign secretary (June)
Outbreak of Spanish Civil War – Italy intervenes
(July)
Formation of German–Italian Axis (October)

1938	German–Austrian *Anschluss* (union)
	Racial laws enacted
	Munich agreement (September)
1939	Chamber of Fasces and Corporations instituted
	Italy annexes Albania (April)
	Pact of Steel (May)
	Outbreak of war – Italy remains neutral (September)
1940	Italy enters war (June)
	Unsuccessful Italian invasion of Greece (October)
1941	Loss of Italian east Africa
	Italy joins German invasion of Russia and declares war on USA
1942	El Alamein
	Allies invade French north Africa
1943	Axis defeat in north Africa
	Strikes in northern Italy (March)
	Mussolini dismisses leading fascists (February–April)
	Allies invade Sicily (July)
	Fascist Grand Council meeting – Mussolini deposed (24–25 July)
	Italian surrender (8 September)
	Mussolini rescued from Gran Sasso (12 September)
	Italy declares war on Germany (October)
	Congress of Verona (November)
1944–5	Allied advance through Italy
1945	Death of Mussolini (28 April)

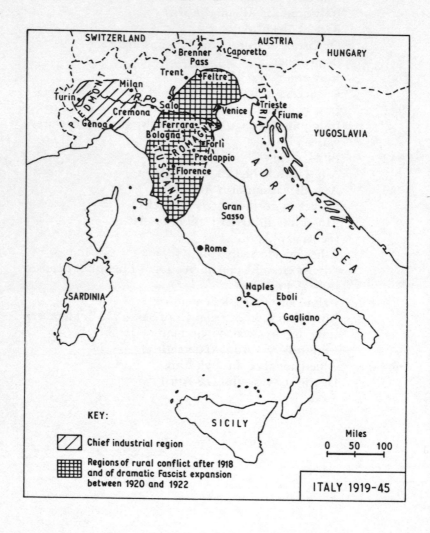

KEY:

▨ Chief industrial region

▩ Regions of rural conflict after 1918
and of dramatic Fascist expansion
between 1920 and 1922

ITALY 1919-45

Miles
0 50 100

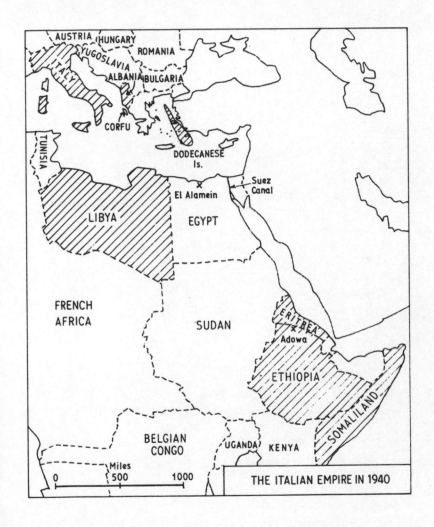

AUSTRIA HUNGARY
YUGOSLAVIA ROMANIA
ITALY ALBANIA BULGARIA
CORFU
DODECANESE Is.
TUNISIA
Suez Canal
LIBYA
EGYPT
El Alamein
FRENCH AFRICA
SUDAN
ERITREA
Adowa
ETHIOPIA
SOMALILAND
BELGIAN CONGO
UGANDA KENYA

Miles
0   500   1000

THE ITALIAN EMPIRE IN 1940

1

Introduction

The present-day visitor to Rome is surrounded by architectural reminders of past centuries and dead regimes: of Republican and Imperial Rome, and of the medieval and Renaissance papacy. Here and there may also be observed traces of another bygone regime, somehow more distant and elusive than any of these; the approach to Italy's Olympic stadium, for example, is along an avenue decorated with defaced stone columns and crumbling mosaics commemorating epoch-making military victories and praising a now-dead leader or *Duce*. The Duce was Benito Mussolini and the regime responsible for thus inscribing his achievements in stone was the fascist regime which ruled Italy between 1922 and 1943.

Fascism aroused violent disagreement among its European contemporaries. Its many admirers, most but by no means all of them on the right of the political spectrum, considered it a spontaneous eruption of patriotic energy which, in power, replaced the fumblings of parliamentary liberalism and the threat of left-wing revolution with order, efficiency and national pride. To its detractors these gains appeared superficial or non-existent; fascism's essential character was seen as one of hooliganism and thuggery in opposition, and repression in power: repression of free speech, free assembly, political parties and trade unions by a corrupt regime and a megalomaniac leader whose purpose increasingly seemed to be that of imperial conquest. Nowadays, although in the English-speaking world discussion of fascism's origins and character may be restricted chiefly to academic circles, in Italy itself the fascist years are still sufficiently recent for academic debate to spill over into the mass media and thereby engage a wider audience.

What was fascism? How and why did it emerge and win power in Italy? How and with what consequences was that power exercised? These are the principal questions that this pamphlet seeks to explore and, where possible, answer. Fascism, it will become clear, cannot be explained entirely in terms of Mussolini himself, vital as his contribution was; nor can it be dismissed as a mere capitalist conspiracy or an irrational outburst of peculiarly 'Latin' violence. A product of the post-war crisis of 1918–22 it may in part have been, yet there is also more to it than this. Fascism, in order to prosper, required a distinctive socio-economic environment, just as in order to challenge for power it needed a political vacuum into which to move. Having attained power, fascism faced chronic domestic problems to which it offered its own, not always novel, solutions, and pursued foreign policies for which it eventually became notorious. In order to understand these and many other aspects of Italian fascism we must first examine the setting within which fascism appeared and from which it was never wholly to escape: the 'liberal' Italy born in 1861.

2

The setting: liberal Italy, 1861–1915

Politics and society in liberal Italy

Between 1859 and 1870 the interaction of nationalist sentiment among limited sections of the population, the influence and involvement of foreign powers, and the ambitions of one Italian state, Piedmont, created a united Italian kingdom. The Risorgimento, as the movement for and achievement of Italian nationhood is commonly known, bequeathed to Italy a complex legacy, of which two threads mainly concern us here: it aroused amongst politically conscious Italians exaggerated expectations concerning Italy's immediate prospects of power and prosperity; and in forging a new nation without involving or satisfying the mass of the population it threw up a socio-political system riddled with potential weaknesses.

The new state, endowed with a limited monarchy, a liberal-parliamentary constitution and a highly centralized adminis-tration, was from the start resented by many as an agent of 'Piedmontization'. National consciousness was uneven and, throughout much of rural, provincial Italy, extremely low; loyalties to fallen dynasties and historic regions persisted, whilst for millions of peasants the only reality was the locality, any outside authority being regarded as an intruder and poten-tial exploiter. Economic and cultural differences aggravated regionalism and localism: much of southern Italy was barren,

3

impoverished and isolated from progressive developments. Metternich had once called Italy a mere 'geographical expression'; now it resembled a mere political expression. As the Piedmontese statesman D'Azeglio remarked, 'We have made Italy – now we must make Italians.'

The gulf between the new Italian state and so many of its people was reflected in and widened by the workings of liberal politics. Late nineteenth-century liberalism was narrowly based: only around half a million male Italians out of a population of approximately 32 million were enfranchised between 1870 and the electoral reform of 1881, whilst between then and the next reform in 1912 the electorate grew from 2 million to 3 million. For three decades after 1870 political office was monopolized by the limited layer of mainly upper-middle-class Italians who had risen to power during the Risorgimento. Increasingly referred to by the revealing term 'political class', these men, divided less by differences of belief or class than by regional loyalties and personal rivalries, treated Italy to a system of parliamentary politics lacking clear party boundaries. Instead, through the practice known as *trasformismo* ('transformism'), premiers and their parliamentary managers fashioned constantly shifting majorities by extending favours to deputies and their constituencies. Elections, both before and after the 1881 reform, were characterized by the bribery, manipulation and outright coercion of voters by local power-cliques and political 'bosses'. Parliament in consequence represented the political class itself and those bound to its members by family, local and economic ties in networks now known as 'clienteles'. Parliament's unrepresentativeness was exacerbated by the attitude of Italian Catholics. The absorption of papal territories into the emergent Italian kingdom during 1860–1, and the final occupation of Rome in 1870, provoked the papacy into adopting a hostile posture towards the new state; for the rest of the century most devout Catholics took no part in politics.

Liberal politics reflected not inaccurately an overwhelmingly rural society distinguished by traditional patterns of agriculture, high illiteracy and low political consciousness. As long as this scene changed only slowly, liberalism was able to function smoothly, if ingloriously. Its test was to come when its gentleman's-club world was challenged by rapid change and new socio-political forces.

4

Hopes that a united Italy would automatically prove internationally powerful were soon dashed. Thoughtful Italians recognized and sometimes resented the important contribution made by other states, especially France and Prussia, to Italy's creation; from this stemmed the acute sensitivity displayed for decades by both politicians and intellectuals concerning Italy's standing as what has been termed 'the least of the great powers'. Although Italy might have done better to settle for the second-class status dictated by her deficient natural resources, her consequent economic backwardness, and the sheer demands of nation-building, the mood generated by the Risorgimento and the climate of intensifying international competitiveness after 1870 ensured that she should instead seek the Great Power status accorded to her fellow 'young' nation, Germany.

Patriotic Italians considered the Risorgimento as incomplete while large numbers of Italian-speakers remained subject to Austrian rule in the regions of Trent and Trieste. The acquisition of these *terre irredente* (unredeemed lands) was the dream of Italian 'irredentists' down to 1918. Successive liberal governments were prevented from pursuing irredentist claims by the implications of Italian ambitions farther afield, in Africa. The presence of large Italian communities in, for example, Tunis and Alexandria, the activities earlier in the century of Italian traders and missionaries, and a pride in the expansionist histories of Rome, Genoa and Venice, helped to convince men like Francesco Crispi, prime minister from 1887 to 1891 and from 1893 to 1896, that Italy must again play an imperial role. The economic case for empire was flimsy; Italy's lack of financial or industrial wealth requiring overseas outlets reduced imperialists to arguing that colonies would *generate* wealth for Italy's own enrichment, end her supposed geo-political 'confinement', and offer millions of Italian emigrants an 'Italian' alternative to South America and the United States. The danger, which they preferred to ignore, was that colonies would be expensive to conquer, defend and police, and that they would run at a loss.

Although most of Italy's early leaders were sceptical regarding her imperial destiny, by the 1880s the tide was flowing against them. During 1881–2, nevertheless, Italian ambitions in north Africa suffered setbacks when France occupied Tunis and

Britain established *de facto* control over Egypt. Only the less succulent prospect of Libya remained to tempt for another thirty years the appetites of Italian 'Africanists'.

Italy's loss of face in north Africa had important consequences. First, annoyance at France's Tunisian coup helped to push Italy into the 1882 Triple Alliance with Germany and her own traditional enemy, Austria-Hungary. Second, imperialist eyes now turned towards east Africa. Eritrea was annexed in 1885, followed in 1889 by part of Somaliland. The goal of imperialists such as Crispi, however, was the establishment of a protectorate over all or part of Ethiopia. Their dreams were destroyed when in 1896 Italian arms suffered a crushing defeat by Ethiopian forces at Adowa, where 5000 Italians were killed and 2000 taken prisoner. In the eyes of many Italians, Adowa discredited not the imperial idea but the liberal system for failing to make it a reality; for them the dream of an east African empire lived on. Forty years after Adowa, fascism was to make it come true.

The challenge of democracy

Beginning in the 1890s, Italy underwent a belated but far-reaching transformation. In agriculture, the backwardness of which had contributed greatly to Italy's general economic retardation, the introduction of capitalist methods and modern machinery created in the fertile Po Valley a new breed of rich *agrari* (agrarians), a numerous class of rural labourers, and a significant intermediate layer of estate managers and technicians; in other regions such as Tuscany the process altered, mainly for the worse, the lives of poor tenant farmers and sharecroppers (peasants who were contractually obliged to surrender to the landlord a proportion, often a half, of their crop or their earnings). In the north-western region bounded by Milan, Turin and Genoa, rapid industrialization at last occurred with the development of heavy industry and its offshoots: iron and steel, metallurgy and engineering, shipbuilding and automobiles, electricity and chemicals. By 1914 there had emerged in the north a powerful class of bankers and industrialists, closely bound to each other and to a protective state. As well as the new, albeit still localized, modern working class produced by industrialization, another 'new' urban class was emerging:

6

increased educational provision in Italy's fast-growing cities and towns was producing a lower middle class eager to fill managerial, bureaucratic and white-collar positions and to keep its distance from the proletariat. The effect of these developments was to alter radically relationships within northern and central Italian society, generating conflicts which in their turn were to contribute massively to the rise of fascism. Economic development affected southern Italy much less than the north and centre. The 'southern problem', shirked by early liberal governments, became if anything more intractable as industrialization and agricultural modernization widened the gap between north and south. For the vast, under-employed rural population of the south an escape was offered by emigration to the Americas or north Africa; by 1914, when Italy's population was 35 million, between 5 and 6 million Italians were living abroad. Much of the south none the less remained economically backward and both socially and politically inert, its people little more than ballot-fodder for the election-rigging which kept liberal politicians in office. Where rapid change did occur, novel political developments naturally followed. Electoral reform in 1881 enfranchised mainly middle-class Italians in urban settings where election-rigging was soon to become more difficult than liberal politicians had anticipated. The result was the election of radical and republican deputies willing to criticize liberal inertia and press for greater parliamentary power. In 1892 the Italian Socialist Party (PSI) was founded; very soon, despite the limitations of the franchise and being banned during the mid-1890s, the party expanded into a significant political force. After the turn of the century socialist (and in some districts anarchist) trade unions attracted increasing support from industrial workers and agricultural labourers, chiefly in northern Italy but also in parts of southern regions such as Sicily and Apulia. This growth occurred against a background, during the 1890s, of widespread and in places bitter social and labour unrest, to which the authorities, especially during the premierships of Crispi and Di Rudinì, responded with a policy of repression. Largely in response to the emerging challenge of a materialistic and 'godless' socialism, Italian Catholics from the turn of the century began to abandon their isolation, participating increasingly in politics and setting up their own trade unions.

For liberalism and parliamentarism to survive, it was vital

that Italy's political system and its leading political figures adapt to these changes. Conservatively inclined liberals were unwilling to accept increasing parliamentary assertiveness or to seek to understand the roots of social distress and disturbances. During the 1890s, and particularly between 1898 and 1900, political and military conservatives sought to bring about a return to a more authoritarian system of government. They failed, owing to their own incompetence and loss of nerve and to the resolute resistance of more genuinely liberal and democratic elements, but the reluctance of conservatives to countenance genuine parliamentary democracy remained evident and ominous.

The new century, however, brought a real attempt to open the liberal system to new currents. Its architect was the dominant liberal statesman of the first twenty years of the century, Giovanni Giolitti. During three pre-war terms as prime minister (November 1903–March 1905, May 1906–December 1909 and March 1911–March 1914), and by exercising powerful influence when out of office, Giolitti sought to accommodate the emergent popular forces of socialism and Catholicism within the parliamentary framework through, respectively, an impartial attitude towards labour disputes and a cooling of traditional liberal anti-clericalism. Even if, as his critics charged, Giolitti was concerned mainly to bolster his own position, his strategy at least offered some chance of involving more Italians in the nation's affairs and of steering liberalism through a period of great change. The growing pragmatism of leading Catholics, and the initially strong tendency towards moderation within the socialist leadership, made the strategy feasible amid the economic buoyancy of 1901–7. In 1912 Giolitti's electoral reform tripled the electorate to almost 9 million, suddenly giving Italy near-universal male suffrage. By now, however, Giolitti's strategy was collapsing. The economic boom slowed from 1907–8, and in 1911 Giolitti committed Italy to the seizure of Libya from the fast-declining Ottoman empire. This appeased conservatives and Nationalists but alienated most socialists and helped strengthen the hand of the PSI's increasingly powerful and vociferous left wing. Among the most militant socialist opponents of the Libyan war was the 28-year-old Benito Mussolini. At the 1912 national congress of the PSI the revolutionary left succeeded in taking over the party organization. Socialist advances at the 1913 elections and subsequent strikes and near-

8

revolutionary activity exposed the limitations of Giolitti's achievement: Italian liberalism had yet to solve the problems presented by the advent of mass politics. The liberals were to have but one more opportunity.

Critics of liberalism

National humiliation and the rise of socialism inspired a vociferous minority of Italian intellectuals to attack liberalism in terms appealing to a growing number of the educated young. The poet Gabriele D'Annunzio, for example, thrilled his readers with his assaults on liberal decadence and his exaltation of violence; and the Futurists, a literary, artistic and semi-political movement led by Filippo Marinetti, extolled physical power, modern technology and war. This restlessness assumed its most political form in Italian Nationalism. Leading figures within the Italian Nationalist Association, founded in 1910, included Enrico Corradini and two future architects of the fascist state, Luigi Federzoni and Alfredo Rocco. Attributing Italy's economic backwardness and low international standing to the weakness and corruption of its political class, the intrinsic defects of liberalism, and the divisive contribution of what Corradini termed 'ignoble socialism', the Nationalists advocated authoritarian government, unrestrained capitalist development, and an imperialist foreign policy. Solidarity among all social classes within a 'proletarian nation' like Italy would, they insisted, make possible the maximization of the country's productive energies and enable it, through imperialism, successfully to challenge 'plutocratic' nations like Britain and France.

Although attracting only modest popular support, chiefly within the educated middle class, the Nationalists established important contacts and influence among conservative politicians, Catholics, and the business community. And, whilst squarely on the political right, they came to occupy common ground with elements of the left. During the first decade of the twentieth century there broke away from the PSI a current known as 'revolutionary syndicalism'. A phenomenon widespread throughout much of Europe before 1914, syndicalism rejected political action via parties and parliaments in favour of revolutionary trade unionism. Italian revolutionary syndicalists such as Edmondo Rossoni challenged the PSI with a strategy in which the trade union would be not only an agent of revolution but also the basis of a new social order. By 1914 some syndicalists had moved further. Convinced that neither the PSI nor the Italian proletariat could achieve revolution, and that the source of Italy's ills was not Italian capitalism – which they now considered insufficiently developed – but the political class, they concluded that the liberal establishment must be overturned by a revolution of all 'productive forces' including the workers *and* the enterprising middle class. This position was not identical with that of the more conservative Nationalists, yet the two groups' shared antagonism towards liberalism and socialism drew them together into an embrace which helped to spawn fascism.

3

The seedbed of fascism

Italy at war

Alone of the leading European participants in the First World War, Italy experienced a public debate over the rival merits of intervention and neutrality: a bitter debate inflicting major damage upon Italy's political fabric. The neutralists comprised the majority of politically conscious Italians – most of the socialists, the Catholics and the Giolittian liberals. The interventionists were a very mixed bunch indeed. On the left they included revolutionary syndicalists, dissident (mainly southern) socialists, and an assortment of radicals, republicans and democrats. For these groups and for others like Marinetti's Futurists, it was vital that Italy commit itself to the forces of progress as represented by the democracies of Britain and France; for the more revolutionary interventionists, Italy's involvement in a major war held the additional attraction that its domestic effects might unleash social and political convulsion and thereby give rise to an entirely new political order. On the right stood conservative liberals and the Nationalists, the latter suppressing their admiration for German authoritarianism in the hope of Italy's acquiring, as the ally of Britain and France, Austrian territory to the north-east and around the Adriatic, as well as Middle-Eastern colonies at the expense of a decaying Turkey. Intervention on the side of Italy's Triple Alliance partners held few such attractions. Many conservatives, like Salandra, prime minister from March 1914, also hoped – in total contrast to the revolutionary left – that participation in what they believed would be a short, victorious war would forge a new solidarity among the increasingly divided people of Italy. During winter and early spring 1914–15 the debate rose in intensity. On 26 April 1915 Italy signed the Treaty of London, committing her to the Anglo-French cause. Parliamentary approval, whilst not constitutionally necessary, was still important before war could be embarked upon; for almost a month, until overwhelming parliamentary support for intervention was given on 20 May, the streets of leading Italian cities rang loud with demonstrations orchestrated by Nationalists and by Futurist- and syndicalist-inspired squads calling themselves Fasci di Azione Rivoluzionaria (Revolutionary Action Groups). Although the word 'fascio', employed to mean a group formed for political purposes, at this stage possessed left-wing connotations, recalling leftist Sicilian *fasci* active during the 1890s, the Fasci di Azione Rivoluzionaria represented the first organized foretaste of the fascism of the 1920s. Their members were to claim credit for Italy's intervention in the war, but in reality the crucial decisions were taken by conservatives such as Prime Minister Salandra and the King, Vittorio Emanuele III.

The war proved a longer and more demanding struggle than most conservative interventionists had anticipated. As left-wing interventionists *had* anticipated, it wrought a profound effect on Italy's society and politics. Some 5.9 million Italian men were conscripted, over 4 million of whom actually went to the war zone on the Italian–Austrian border. Casualties were high: over half a million killed, 600,000 captured and a million wounded, of whom 450,000 were permanently disabled. Italy's infantrymen were mostly peasant conscripts, many torn for the first time from their native region to serve a country of whose interests they were only barely aware. Consequently few can have felt much enthusiasm for the Italian cause, and as time passed their resentfulness grew, both towards the distant governing class that had sent them to the front with little or no promise of ultimate material reward and, in many cases, towards the neutralist PSI and the mainly exempted industrial workers it represented. Grievances also existed higher up the social and military hicrarchy. Some 140,000 new officers were created during the war, mostly from among educated young middle-class Italians. Many of these, whatever their initial attitude towards the war, developed at the front a strong sense of comradeship, identification with the war effort and with expansionist war-aims, and mistrust of the politicians at home, which were to have important peacetime repercussions.

War also brought profound changes to Italy herself. Most significant was the rapid growth and increased concentration of those industries most closely linked with war production: metallurgy, engineering, shipbuilding and automobiles. Any suggestion of a lasting boom was nevertheless misleading, for Italy's war machine consumed industrial products of a kind and at a rate no peacetime economy was likely to match. This was all the more serious in view of the accompanying growth and increased unionization of the industrial working class. A distorted economy, potentially short of raw materials and export outlets and unable to benefit from a healthy domestic market, was a sure recipe for post-war difficulties. Returning troops, who would be among the principal sufferers in such a situation, would hardly be mollified at seeing others who had got rich while they were at the front: not only financial and industrial profiteers but also ambitious peasants who had seized opportunities to buy more land. Meanwhile, the political situation looked more and more discouraging. With the neutralist Giolitti on the sidelines, three wartime premiers – Salandra, Paolo Boselli and Orlando – struggled unconvincingly to conduct government without him. To many Italians, liberal government was coming to seem ineffectual and irrelevant.

The crisis of Italy's war came in October 1917 with her calamitous defeat at Caporetto. In a few weeks 10,000 Italian troops died, 300,000 were wounded, and 300,000 captured by the Austrians, whose army drove seventy miles into Italian – and former Austrian – territory. The defeat, though reversed in the dying weeks of the war at Vittorio Veneto, shocked Italian public opinion, produced an unprecedented rallying to the war effort, and galvanized the government into an overdue propaganda campaign. The politicians' commitment to democracy was re-affirmed and Italy's peasant troops were belatedly promised land and improved treatment when the war ended. Another event, occurring simultaneously with Caporetto, may well have stimulated the politicians' resolve: the Bolshevik revolution in Russia.

The post-war crisis

Italy's post-war condition soon made nonsense of any optimism generated by official propaganda during 1918. Her economy was afflicted by a succession of overlapping crises: food and raw material shortages during 1918–19; acute inflation, beginning during the war and continuing down to 1921; and, as 2.5 million demobilized ex-servicemen returned home from early 1920, rapidly rising unemployment.

Italy's political system was confronted with these problems at a time when it also faced the sudden advent of an age of mass politics to which its practices and personnel were ill-attuned. In fulfilment of wartime democratic promises, proportional representation, favouring modern parties over traditional patronage politics, was introduced for the 1919 elections. The two largest parties to emerge from the contest were the PSI and the Partito Popolare Italiano, a Catholic party founded in 1919 with the approval of the Vatican but officially independent of it; the party's leader was a priest, Luigi Sturzo. The future of Italian democracy now lay largely in the hands of these two mass parties; neither was strong enough to govern alone, yet despite common ground between moderate socialists and left-wing *popolari*, the mutual antagonism of the socialist left and the Catholic right prevented a reformist alliance which might have guided Italy into a genuinely democratic era. Power, or its shadow, thus reverted by default to the old liberal cliques, four of whose members – Nitti, Giolitti, Bonomi and Facta – occupied the premiership between the end of the war and October 1922. These three years were to show how limited were the liberal leaders' capacities for coping with a transformed political environment.

Two overriding issues made post-war government difficult: social unrest and nationalist grievance. Strikes and 'illegal' occupations began to affect both industry and agriculture during the last year of the war and reached a peak during the *biennio rosso* (two red years) of 1918–20. Trade union membership rose steeply in this period, that of the socialist CGL (General Confederation of Labour) from 250,000 to over 2 million and that of the Catholic unions from 160,000 to 1.16 million. Militancy channelled by both socialists and, in the countryside, left-wing *popolari* involved factory workers, rural labourers and poor

14

peasants throughout northern and central Italy. The bitterest conflicts arose in the industrial north-west and in the agricultural regions of Emilia-Romagna and Tuscany. Many conservative Italians interpreted the unrest not as the product of accelerated long-term change and immediate post-war hardship, but as the start of 'bolshevik' revolution. The revolutionary bluster of the socialist left certainly encouraged such fears, yet the lack of genuine revolutionary leadership and of Soviet instigation made revolution unlikely. The *biennio rosso*'s climax came in August 1920 when workers occupied factories and shipyards in several cities of northen Italy; when the occupations collapsed, the tide of worker and peasant militancy began to ebb.

The opportunity for counter-attack now presented itself to the well-to-do *agrari* and industrial employers. No longer, in the changed world of post-war Italy, prepared to accept the impartiality towards labour disputes observed by most governments since 1901, landowning and industrial interests began to seek a new way of ordering the three-way relationship of capital, labour and the state. The anti-socialism of the rich was shared, moreover, by innumerable less well-off Italians, alienated by the socialists' monopolizing of employment opportunities in districts under their control and even more, perhaps, by the socialist left's ill-judged, vocal and sometimes violent antagonism towards war veterans of all classes.

The emotional commitment of many ex-servicemen – and other nationalistically inclined Italians – to the wartime struggle and its aims helped to fuel the post-war governments' second set of problems. Italy's gains in 1919 were far from negligible. Her traditional foe, Austria-Hungary, was dismembered and Italy's north-eastern frontier advanced to the Brenner Pass, whilst at the head of the Adriatic she annexed the city of Trieste and much of Istria. What she did not receive, giving rise to the myth of a 'mutilated victory', were African and Middle-Eastern colonies and additional territory around the Adriatic. One Adriatic city, Fiume, became a *cause célèbre* when in September 1919 it was seized from its temporary four-power occupying forces by a band of Italian war-veterans led by the poet-adventurer D'Annunzio. For over a year D'Annunzio's 'regency' held Fiume, defying international order and lauded by nationalist zealots and non-socialist revolutionaries throughout Italy. The 'style'

15

of D'Annunzio's regime, with its processions, sloganizing and balcony harangues, established a model which fascism was later to embrace; so, too, did its promulgation of a 'producers' state'. By the time Giolitti finally expelled D'Annunzio from Fiume in December 1920, the revolutionary poet had become the hero and leader-in-waiting of Italians anxious to repair the insult of 'mutilated victory' and to destroy liberalism without succumbing to 'bolshevism'. Another such Italian, overshadowed as yet by D'Annunzio, was Benito Mussolini.

The making of a fascist

Benito Mussolini was born in 1883 near Predappio, a small town in the Romagna. The regional tradition of rebelliousness was well represented by his father, a republican and socialist blacksmith whose outlook and temperament Mussolini largely inherited. An undistinguished and disorderly educational career, blotted by several acts of violence, nevertheless ended with Mussolini qualifying in 1902 as a schoolmaster. From then until 1910 he led a varied existence. Two periods of unsuccessful schoolteaching were interrupted by two years (1902–4) in Switzerland as a casual labourer and occasional vagrant, and another two years (1904–6) back in Italy on military service. From 1908 onwards he began to find his true niche, that of a left-wing journalist, first in Austrian-ruled Trent and then in the Romagna town of Forlì. As editor of the local socialist newspaper and secretary of the town's socialist organization from 1910, Mussolini was able to establish in Forlì a personal base within the PSI from which to leap to national prominence in 1911–12 as a leading spokesman of the party's radical wing, opposed to war in Libya and co-operation with Giolitti. One of the authors of the PSI's leftward lurch between 1910 and 1914, Mussolini, as editor from 1912 of the leading socialist daily, *Avanti* of Milan, initially adhered dutifully to his party's official line by opposing Italian intervention in the European war. By October 1914, however, he had moved to a position of 'active neutrality' sympathetic to France and Britain, and late in the year openly espoused intervention. As a result he was forced to resign his editorship of *Avanti* and was then expelled from the PSI. His allies in the interventionist cause were now revolutionary syndicalists, Futurists, radical

16

republicans and right-wing Nationalists: the bizarre coalition out of which he was later to forge fascism.

Why a socialist and internationalist, such as Mussolini still appeared to be shortly before the war began, should so swiftly have become an advocate of patriotic war remains uncertain. His earlier socialism was perfectly genuine in its way, as advertised by his enthusiastic support for strikers in Forlì; so, as far as it is possible to judge, was his outspoken condemnation of nationalism. His socialism was nevertheless of a highly personal, even idiosyncratic kind, Marxian in theory yet closer in spirit to revolutionary syndicalism or the insurrectionary republicanism of his native region. For all his anti-nationalism, moreover, his horizons remained essentially Italian; his unforced return from Switzerland for military service and his exemplary term as a soldier hint at a layer of barely conscious patriotism beneath the outward internationalism. The key to his political career, perhaps, is that it was the Italy around him that he detested and with whose political system and political class he refused to identify. The principal target of the hatred which made him a socialist was liberal Italy's narrow ruling class as much as the capitalist system, and his goal revolution itself rather than the particular kind of post-revolutionary society desired by most fellow socialists. Events at home and abroad during 1913–14 persuaded Mussolini, like the revolutionary syndicalists, that the Marxian analysis was inappropriate to Italy. Within Italy, the practical limits of socialist militancy, culminating in the insurrectionary failure of 'Red Week' in June 1914, convinced him that neither his party nor the Italian working class was capable of revolution. Elsewhere, the behaviour of workers throughout Europe during 1914 undermined his previous belief in international working-class solidarity and impressed him with the potency of nationalism as a popular force. Influenced by this double revelation, Mussolini gradually embraced the left-wing interventionist view that Italy's participation in the war would generate a revolution of non-Marxian type which would nevertheless overturn the liberal system and bring a new ruling class to power. It was this revolution to which he now dedicated himself.

The immediate prospects did not, however, look good. Although soon able to launch a new paper, the *Il Popolo d'Italia* ('The Italian People'), with money from fellow interventionists and from the French, Mussolini sank into insignificance once the war itself began to preoccupy public attention. Two years of war service – he was invalided out – were followed by a return to journalism. Restored to the editorial chair of *Il Popolo d'Italia*, Mussolini devoted the next two years to developing and propagating a new, and in the long run highly shrewd, strategy of national revolution. By the end of the war *Il Popolo d'Italia* had abandoned its original claim still to be socialist and was declaring itself the voice of 'producers and soldiers' against parasitic liberals and unpatriotic socialists. For the present, it was a voice to which few listened. With the war over and the socialists in the ascendant, Mussolini the socialist renegade lay stranded on the margins of Italian political life. He was not, however, to remain there for long.

4

The conquest of power, 1919–25

Urban fascism and agrarian fascism, 1919–21

On 23 March 1919 the almost forgotten Mussolini presided over the foundation in Milan of a new political movement, the Fascio di Combattimento (Combat Group). The 118 people present at this obscure event comprised mainly war veterans, Futurists and dissident leftists like Mussolini himself. The movement's name harked back to the interventionist Fasci di Azione Rivoluzionaria of 1915, which Mussolini had vainly hoped to keep together as a vehicle for post-war revolution. The term *fascio*, once the preserve of the left, was by now commoner on the right, for whose devotees it connoted the *fasces*, the bound rods borne by the magistracy of Republican Rome, and the notion of 'strength through unity'.

The new movement nevertheless projected itself as a left-wing challenger for the working-class support of socialism. Its programme was republican, anti-clerical and democratic, calling for decentralization, female suffrage and proportional representation, the confiscation of excess war profits, worker participation in all industrial management and worker control of public services, the nationalization of the arms industry, a minimum wage and an eight-hour day, and the repudiation of imperialism. What eventually proved most significant about this programme was its negligible impact: in the November 1919

19

elections the fascists in Milan – their only sizeable base – polled under 5000 votes out of 275,000 cast. By December 1919, with many leftists already abandoning the movement and D'Annunzio eclipsing Mussolini as the likely leader of 'national syndicalism', fascism faced collapse. Mussolini held on, however, with some support from wealthy Milanese who sensed fascism's anti-socialist potential, and from summer 1920 the movement entered a new and crucial phase in its development.

The most important element in fascism's revival was the growth of 'agrarian' fascism throughout much of northern and central Italy, most notably the Po Valley and Tuscany where, especially since 1918, socialist unions and Catholic peasant leagues had come to threaten the power of the *agrari* and the position and status of such 'middling' elements as richer peasants, estate managers and the provincial urban professional class. Fascist nuclei in provincial capitals such as Bologna, Ferrara and Florence inaugurated a policy of *squadrismo*, involving violence by fascist squads (It. *squadre*, sing. *squadra*) against the organizations, installations and militants of socialism and trade unionism. Initially on a small scale, these activities expanded as early success attracted new members to the *fasci*. Over the next two years fascist punitive expeditions became commonplace. The offices of left-wing parties, socialist unions and Catholic peasant leagues, as well as left-wing newspaper offices and printing shops, were sacked and frequently burnt down; physical violence and humiliation, through the use of clubs, knives and guns, and the forced consumption of castor oil, were meted out to left-wing and trade-union activists. *Squadrismo*, which often enjoyed the benevolence of police authorities and the participation of off-duty policemen, worked wonders. Between autumn 1920 and summer 1922 the organizational structure of socialist and Catholic rural trade-unionism was destroyed across much of central and northern Italy. While strikes and union membership dramatically declined, *fasci* proliferated and their membership increased; by 1922 most provinces outside the south possessed an extensive fascist organization headed by a *ras* (an Ethiopian word for chieftain). The *ras*, men from a variety of backgrounds such as Roberto Farinacci of Cremona, Dino Grandi of Bologna and Italo Balbo of Ferrara, commanded great authority within their own districts and operated all but independently of Mussolini. Although

20

still relatively weak in the south, fascism, which only two years before had been reduced to under 1000 members, by mid-1922 numbered over 250,000 nationally.

Fascism was now revealing its distinctive social character. Fascist leaders and activists were recruited from among war veterans, especially former junior officers and NCOs; from the educated middle-class youth, professionals and white-collar workers in towns and cities; and in the countryside from the upper and middling layers of rural society – landowners, better-off peasant proprietors and tenant farmers, estate managers and, most important, their sons. Genuinely spontaneous support from the urban workers and poorer peasants whom fascism had originally sought to attract was meagre, but as the left's organizations crumbled many poorer peasants and some workers joined fascism and its newly forming unions out of sheer self-preservation. Increasingly, moral and financial support, if not always actual membership, was coming from rich *agrari* and, to a lesser extent, industrialists eager to see fascism crush or irreversibly weaken trade unionism and socialism.

What these growing numbers of fascists sought from fascism is difficult to state briefly. For some who had fought in the war and others too young to have done so, fascism offered comradeship and excitement in a dull and ungrateful post-war world; for the more politically conscious it represented a continuation of the war in peacetime, Italy's enemies now being socialist and liberal 'traitors'; for many more, fascism promised the revolutionary overthrow of liberal Italy's tired ruling caste by a new élite, broadly middle class in composition, steeled in battle against Italy's foreign and internal enemies, and thereby qualified to govern.

The March on Rome

As fascism flourished and became more unambiguously reactionary, in its role if not necessarily its rhetoric and self-image, its appeal to 'respectable' opinion increased. Liberals were not immune: at the May 1921 elections the *fasci di combattimento*, although not actually a political party, joined Giolitti's anti-socialist 'national' bloc. The thirty-five fascist deputies elected took their seats on the far right of the chamber. Fascism's rightward momentum was irresistible; when in summer 1921

Mussolini, still reluctant to sever totally his links with the left, sought to reach a truce with the socialists, his own movement prevented it and the undeclared civil war between fascists and socialists continued. In November 1921 any doubts regarding fascism's political direction and thirst for power vanished when the movement became a political party, the Partito Nazionale Fascista (PNF), with a frankly rightist programme embracing monarchism, free trade and anti-socialism.

Within a year Mussolini was prime minister of Italy. Despite the 'revolutionary' myth of the fascist March on Rome in October 1922, fascism owed its accession to power largely to conservative forces. During 1922 the conviction formed in political circles, within the Vatican and the Catholic hierarchy, among 'liberal' intellectuals and journalists, and among industrialists and *agrari*, that fascism must be given its political chance. Not only Giolitti but also his conservative rival Salandra, the Prime Minister Facta and other leading liberals now wished to form governments with fascist participation – hoping that through office fascism might be tamed, 'transformed' and reabsorbed into the liberal system. Liberal politicians were incapable of collaborating with any but the most moderate socialists or with Sturzo and the *popolari*. Bereft of any new ideas, they therefore succumbed to the attractions of an accommodation with fascism. Outside the political world, businessmen and *agrari*, impressed by fascism's highly practical anti-socialism, expected fascist participation in government to stiffen official attitudes towards labour; intellectuals and academics hoped fascism would inject new vigour into an exhausted body politic; and the Vatican, especially after the election of Pope Pius XI in February 1922, was led to expect an end to the church–state feud and important concessions to the church should fascists enter the government.

Although few of these conservative interests thought further than fascist participation in an otherwise conventional government, growing belief in the indispensability of such participation weakened their resistance to the more far-reaching takeover of power that most leading fascists now had in mind. Following an unsuccessful anti-fascist general strike, launched by the socialists in August 1922, fascist pressure intensified; in October plans for an insurrectionary march on Rome began to be laid. Bluff was all-important. Despite fascism's popular support, no more than 30,000 activists, mostly ill-armed, were available for the march, which would easily be squashed were the government to resist and the army, as was to be expected, to obey the royal command. Either physical defeat or craven retreat would probably have burst the fascist bubble. In the event the established powers smoothed Mussolini's path. With fascists mobilizing in the provinces the Prime Minister, Facta, determined on resistance and on 27 October requested the King's signature to a decree of martial law obliging the army to meet the expected march. Having at first agreed, the King on the following morning changed his mind; his reasons remain unclear, though he may well have been concerned about fascist sympathies within the army, fearful of civil war, and fatalistic regarding the inevitability of fascism's entry into government. Facta promptly resigned; Mussolini refused to join any government he did not lead and on 29 October was rewarded with the premiership. Only then did the March on Rome take place.

The road to dictatorship, 1922–5

Italy now had a fascist prime minister but not, strictly speaking, a fascist government. For two years Mussolini presided over coalition governments from which, of the major parties, only the socialists and, later, the *popolari* were excluded. The future in October 1922 was utterly uncertain, no clear agreement existing among fascists and their supporters as to whether fascism implied something temporary or permanent, eventual 'normalization' or a genuine revolution.

Mussolini certainly had no wish to relinquish the power he now held, probably envisaging a drastic revision of the existing system to ensure the repeated renewal of his authority rather than a complete political revolution. This would have satisfied his conservative supporters, for whom a fascist-led government may have been a blessing but the prospect of an outright fascist regime remained disturbing. For most conservatives the ideal was a 'normalization' of politics once the balance of power had tilted decisively against the left, the unions and the lower classes. Until then they would not exercise the power they still possessed to unseat Mussolini. The dream of 'normalization' was shared by liberal politicians, who refused to make serious moves against Mussolini in the hope that he might stumble and

23

the way back be reopened to them. For them, however, times were changing ominously, as their local clienteles, especially in the south, deserted them for fascism. Ostensibly more threatening to Mussolini were the *popolari* and the left. The former, however, largely disintegrated after first being dropped from the government in 1923 and then abandoned by the pro-fascist Vatican, whilst the left was weakened by the continuing attacks of fascist squads, the loss of trade union membership, and divisions among moderates, radicals and communists.

Until the summer of 1924 the initiative thus lay with fascism, though not always with Mussolini. Fascism was now a fluid alliance, within which five strands stood out: the *ras* and *squadristi*, eager for a 'second revolution' bringing greater power to themselves and the social layers they represented, yet unclear or unconcerned as to the actual purpose of power; the fascist 'left', ex-syndicalists like Rossoni and Michele Bianchi, who wished fascism to supersede the 'old' left and construct a 'national-syndicalist' state capable of stimulating popular energies and enthusiasm; fascist 'technocrats' such as Giuseppe Bottai who saw fascism as an élitist, modernizing force; the Nationalists, whose association merged with the PNF in 1923 in the hope of guiding it in a pro-capitalist and imperialist direction; and conservative fascists desirous of 'normalization' and defence of the socio-political status quo. Mussolini's most serious problems came from the *squadristi*, for in the far from monolithic PNF much of the real power rested not at the top but in the hands of provincial bosses. Their demands for a full-scale fascist takeover embarrassed a Mussolini anxious to move cautiously in his relations with conservative forces. Whilst wishing to tighten control over the *ras* and their disorderly followers, he needed this self-same disorderliness as a warning to enemies and false friends of what might happen if they misbehaved. By unifying the *squadristi* into a national fascist militia and creating a Fascist Grand Council to bring the *ras* under his supposed control, Mussolini went some way, but not far, towards creating a more disciplined party.

Mussolini's determination to strengthen fascism's position was soon evident with the passage in July 1923 of an electoral reform, the Acerbo Law, designed to give the leading party or alliance at a general election two-thirds of the seats in parliament. At the April 1924 election the official, fascist-led list of candidates polled 66 per cent of the votes and won 374 out of 535 seats. In the south, where fascism had been weak before October 1922, the movement was now able to use the customary election-rigging machinery in order to ensure a triumph for the official list; in the north, on the other hand, the contest remained sufficiently free for the left to poll too well for the government's comfort, demonstrating that even in its own strongholds fascism's grip was not yet total.

The elections had been accompanied by unprecedented fascist violence, which provoked bitter opposition protests when parliament re-opened. The fascists, both inside and outside parliament, were now bent on making things difficult for their critics. One of the most outspoken was a moderate socialist, Giacomo Matteotti; in June 1924 he was seized by a gang of fascists and stabbed to death, his body remaining undiscovered until August. When the fascist thugs' guilt was exposed, Mussolini's moral if not actual complicity was inescapable.

The Matteotti crisis proved crucial to the development of a fascist regime. Amidst a wave of anti-fascist sentiment, much of the socialist, Catholic and democratic opposition withdrew from parliament in protest: the so-called 'Aventine secession'. Mussolini panicked and would have resigned had the King required it. The King did not, demonstrating the unwillingness of conservatives even now to abandon Mussolini, partly from fear of a left-wing revival and partly in the hope of exploiting Mussolini's vulnerability in order to increase their influence over him. Without conservative help the opposition, and liberals like Giolitti who belatedly joined it late in 1924, were powerless. Mussolini thus retained office, but now faced mutiny within his own party. The *ras*, now officially known as 'consuls', saw the crisis as justifying not concession to opposition but its elimination. In December 1924 they collectively demanded that Mussolini, on pain of deposition as leader of fascism, move decisively towards a dictatorship. On 3 January 1925 Mussolini made it plain to what remained of parliament that this was now his intention.

5
Mussolini's dictatorship

1925
leggi fascistissime

Duce, party and state

During 1925–6 the dictatorship was cemented, a process punctuated by four unsuccessful but highly convenient attempts on Mussolini's life. The total power effectively granted Mussolini by a law of December 1925 was reinforced by a battery of repressive measures. Political opposition and free trade unions were banned; the free press surrendered to a combination of censorship and fascist takeover; elected local governments were replaced by appointed officials; and the essentials of a police state were created by extending the government's powers of arrest and detention, increasing the scope of the death penalty, introducing a special court for political 'crimes', and forming a 'secret' police force, the OVRA.

These and other measures increased the power not of the fascist party but of the state and the Duce (leader), as Mussolini was coming to be officially known. Their principal architects were two ex-Nationalist fascists: Federzoni, minister of the interior until November 1926, and Rocco, minister of justice from 1925 to 1932. In obstructing a party takeover of the state they enjoyed Mussolini's support but antagonized elements in the fascist party itself. The PNF's condition remained fluid. Its most vociferous members were the intransigent *squadristi*, whose most conspicuous representative was Roberto Farinacci.

26

Viewing fascism in 'populist' terms involving constant assemblies, rallies and punitive activities, and nursing a belief in the quasi-mystical, pseudo-democratic bond between leaders and led, these militants now yearned for a fascist capture of the state and especially of its repressive apparatus. The raucousness and violence of this element repelled other fascists: ex-syndicalists whose interest lay in developing fascist unions rather than the party; and sophisticated technocrats such as Bottai who wished the party to function as a nursery for future Italian leaders. Probably more numerous than all of these were those who had been mounting the fascist bandwagon since 1920 for conservative or opportunistic reasons and for whom the party meant little more than a means of self-advancement.

In January 1925 Mussolini appointed Farinacci to the post of party secretary. The move proved an astute one, especially since the Duce detested Farinacci personally and held totally different views concerning the desirable relationship of party to state. For even as Farinacci continued to press for a fascist takeover, his centralization of the party was simultaneously destroying the power and independence of provincial bosses like himself and neutralizing the *squadrismo* of which he was the chief spokesman. By the time he was manoeuvred into resigning in April 1926 his job was done and the party well on the way to being tamed. The PNF's new orderliness was enshrined officially in the revised Party Statute of October 1926, whereby the Duce became explicitly head of the party for the first time; the Fascist Grand Council retained the theoretical power to formulate policy; and, most important, all party posts became subject to appointment rather than election. During the late 1920s and early 1930s the party's subservience to the state, expressly required by Mussolini, became increasingly evident, assisted by repeated purges of 'old-guard' intransigents carried out by Farinacci's successors in the post of party secretary, Augusto Turati (1926–30) and Giovanni Giuriati (1930–1); during their terms of office, perhaps as many as 170,000 fascists, mainly of the 'old guard' variety, were expelled from the PNF. Party office now fell more and more into the hands of those who, like Bottai and Turati himself, desired a highly professionalized party capable, if not of swallowing the state, then at least of creating a new ruling class.

Turati and Giuriati were nevertheless frustrated in their

pursuit of an active, dedicated, professionalized party; by the mid-1930s the PNF, with a membership of 1,400,000 by the end of 1933 (by 1939 it had reached over 2,600,000), had become an inflated bureaucracy of time-serving careerists, largely devoid of a creative political role. Achille Starace, party secretary for most of the decade (1931–9), was a truly representative figure: utterly deferential towards Mussolini and concerned with propaganda and parades rather than political or social initiatives. The party's condition was reflected in the social flavour of its membership. Whereas in 1921–2 perhaps a third of PNF members were workers and peasants, by the late 1920s it was an organization overwhelmingly of insecure and ambitious public employees, professionals and white-collar workers; in parts of the south public employees made up 75–80 per cent of members. Farinacci's fear that the party, if deprived of the vitality of *squadrismo*, would lapse into a cosy middle age, was wholly borne out.

Fascist Italy may thus have been a one-party state, but it was not a 'party-state' such as Soviet Russia or even Nazi Germany. This does not mean, however, that the PNF's role within the regime was unimportant. Quite apart from providing job opportunities for the Italian lower middle class, the party came to perform numerous vital administrative and politically educative tasks: it attempted to raise Italy's youth in the spirit of fascism; through the elaborate bureaucracy of the Dopolavoro ('After-work') organization it supervised the leisure and social activities of the working population, seeking to compensate workers for their falling wages with a variety of fringe benefits and in the process to 'cure' them of socialism; and it created a distinctive 'climate' through the mounting of rallies, sports events and other propaganda-filled activities.

Power nevertheless resided elsewhere: in the traditional apparatus of the state – to which, moreover, the police system remained subordinate; in autonomous centres of influence such as private industry and the church; and of course in the Duce, an essential ingredient of whose role was his ability to deal personally and separately with these interests. Mussolini's preference for state over party and his taste for personal power were manifested by his own tenure of several ministries. From 1926 he occupied the interior ministry continuously, whilst between 1926 and 1929 he held no fewer than eight ministries himself.

The rising cult of the Duce did not therefore mislead: by the 1930s Mussolini's regime was as personal as propaganda suggested. Whether or not it was also, as that same propaganda claimed, 'totalitarian' will be considered later.

The theory and reality of the Corporate State

Italian fascism's chief claim to political creativity lay in the construction between 1925 and 1939 of the Corporate State, a system purporting to be revolutionary yet socially unifying, to guarantee economic progress and social justice by bringing employers, managers and workers together within a legally constituted framework. Fascist corporativism aroused genuine interest abroad. Numerous foreign academic political scientists, particularly in the United States, published books examining its supposed workings, while its many political admirers and would-be emulators included the British fascist leader Sir Oswald Mosley, and Juan Domingo Perón, future dictator of Argentina.

Corporativism was not the invention of fascism, however. Its pedigree was long and complex, two main strands requiring mention here. One descended from nineteenth-century Catholic ideas concerning modern society. Socially concerned Catholics such as Pope Leo XIII (1878–1903), holding society to be naturally harmonious and the growing social conflict of the day therefore curable, sought to bring together employers and workers in each area of economic activity within 'mixed unions' or 'corporations'. Thus, for example, all agriculturalists, from the largest landowner to the poorest farmhand, would belong to one 'corporation', and all factory owners, plant managers and workers to another. These bodies, it was argued, not only would replace class conflict with class co-operation but might also replace geographical constituencies and ideological differences as the basis of parliamentary representation. The second strand was that of syndicalism, with its stress on trade unions as agents of revolution and of future social and political organization. Syndicalists embraced corporativism in abandoning the idea of class conflict in favour of class collaboration to increase industrial production – an idea, increasingly termed 'productivism', which in 1919–20 was incorporated into the constitution of D'Annunzio's Fiume republic. The Italian Nationalists borrowed

29

from both Catholic corporativism and syndicalism in formulating their own theories, whereby corporations would be used to enhance capitalist wealth and state authority.

Corporativist ideas were thus widely held, if often vaguely grasped, among early fascists. Between 1919 and 1925 their most enthusiastic advocates were ex-syndicalists like Bianchi and Rossoni, head of the Fascist Labour Confederation until 1928. Where 'party men' such as Farinacci wished the fascist *party* to dominate Italy, Rossoni and the fascist 'left' sought to achieve popular identification with the Italian state through 'national syndicalism'. This would involve employers and fascist unions coming together within 'integrated corporations' designed to control labour relations, determine economic policies and channel public opinion. Other fascists viewed corporativism differently. The 'moderate' Bottai, for example, saw it as a rational means of peacefully eliminating class conflict, boosting production, and altogether 'modernizing' Italy through a kind of 'managerial revolution'. To ex-Nationalists like Rocco, however, it meant little more than a way of disciplining labour in the interest of employers.

Until 1925 the fascist 'left' forced the pace, though with limited success owing to the continued competition of the still-active free unions and the unwillingness of employers, especially those organized in the Confindustria (Confederation of Industry), to accept 'integral corporativism'. The Chigi Palace Pact of December 1923, between Confindustria and the Fascist Labour Confederation, promised the latter exclusive bargaining rights with employers in return for surrendering its corporativist ambitions; in the event the employers failed to keep their side of the bargain. The rapid erosion of support for the socialist and Catholic unions after January 1925 revitalized the Fascist Labour Confederation and inspired a new agreement with Confindustria, the Vidoni Palace Pact of October 1925, whereby the two sides recognized each other as the sole representatives respectively of labour and capital.

For Rossoni and the ex-syndicalist fascists the stage now seemed set for an advance to 'integral corporativism' and the desired institutionalized partnership between capital and labour. Over the next two years they were to be sorely disappointed. Even as the membership of the Fascist Labour Confederation swelled with former members of the now illegal socialist and

30

Catholic unions, the reality of the regime's attitude towards labour relations became apparent. Rocco's labour relations law of April 1926 and the much-trumpeted Labour Charter of 1927 brought the fascist unions firmly under state control and installed a labour-relations system decidedly favourable to employers. In 1928 the Fascist Labour Confederation, now almost 3 million strong, was broken up into six parts, depriving Rossoni of his power base and effectively extinguishing fascist syndicalism as a serious force.

Official commitment to some sort of corporativism was nevertheless embodied in the Ministry of Corporations set up in July 1926. Over the next thirteen years the Corporate State came unsteadily into being. In 1930, with Bottai as minister of corporations, a potential corporative parliament was introduced in the form of a National Council of Corporations. Four years later the long-promised 'mixed corporations' of employers and employees were finally created: twenty-two of them, each ostensibly empowered to determine wages and conditions within a specific area of economic activity (for example textiles, grain production, the merchant marine, etc.). Lastly, in 1939, a full-scale Chamber of Fasces and Corporations was inaugurated in place of the moribund parliament. It had been a long journey, but the Corporate State was now a reality.

Or was it? Even if corporativism did offer a rational alternative to the conflicts within capitalist society, the Italian attempt to implement it, for all the enthusiasm of the syndicalists and the sincere efforts of Bottai and others, was never a serious one. Once the early thrust of fascist syndicalism had been blunted and any serious prospect of a 'worker-based' version of fascism destroyed, important decisions came to be taken in the employers' favour. From 1928 the workers' side within the corporate structures was manned not by genuine workers or their chosen representatives but by fascist officials, usually – though not invariably – amenable towards employers. The latter, on the other hand, were able to defend their interests effectively not only *within* the corporations but also by dealing directly with the government through surviving autonomous bodies such as *Confindustria*. Corporativism in practice, especially during the depression of the 1930s, thus represented a means of disciplining labour in the interests of employers and of the state.

Mussolini's personal responsibility in this was considerable. Although before 1925 he had sometimes toyed with the idea of a fascism based on the power of labour, whenever confronted with employer resistance, either to labour pressure or, as between 1930 and 1934, to the possibility of genuine corporativist advances, he backed down. For the Duce corporativism was a matter of pragmatism, not of principle: a theory to which most fascists could subscribe, over which indeed they could even be permitted to engage in limited debate; an apparent social and political experiment useful for bestowing respectability on his regime in the eyes of foreigners; and an elaborate facade behind which corruption and exploitation could flourish while Mussolini himself pursued the very different goals which, by the 1930s, interested him far more.

6

Italy under fascism

Fascist economic policies and their impact

Fascism was not an economic system. Throughout its existence it retained a largely rhetorical anti-capitalist strand derived from its left-wing origins, but following Mussolini's early compromise with big business and *agrari* this was never allowed significantly to influence policy. Mussolini himself knew little of economics and possessed only generalized economic ideas. By 1922 his views, like those of many fascists, amounted to little more than a commitment to 'productivism': to precisely what end was as yet unclear.

Rejecting the destruction of capitalism, fascism was thus forced to function within an inherited economic framework. The ground rules of what passed for fascist economic policies were laid by such dominant characteristics of the Italian economy, clearly visible even before the war, as the close bonds between state and heavy industry, the selective favouring by governments of some interests at the expense of others, and a weak consumer sector caused by the state's attempts to divert personal incomes, through taxation, into industrial investment.

Even to talk of 'fascist' economic policies before 1925 would be inappropriate. Italy was simply permitted to share in Europe's post-war boom, thanks to the *laissez-faire* policies pursued by Mussolini and his finance minister De Stefani. Only during

33

1925–6, with the dictatorship in the process of creation, did serious inflation, balance of payments difficulties, and a depreciating lira force De Stefani's replacement by Giuseppe Volpi, an industrialist and banker, whose deflationary and protectionist policies set the tone for the rest of the fascist era. At the personal instigation of Mussolini, for whom it was a matter of national pride, the lira was in 1927 fixed at the artificially high level of 90 to the pound sterling – the 'Quota 90' of fascist propaganda. High tariff barriers were erected to protect heavy industry and selected agricultural products; during the late 1920s and the 1930s, Italy's industrial and agricultural exporting sector was largely sacrificed in favour of a sluggish domestic economy stabilized by cartels and price-fixing. General deflation, wage-cutting and the suppression of free trade unions not only implied the rejection of a vigorous domestic market but also indicated fascism's social priorities, principally a preference for stability over mobility.

Whilst plainly damaging to some sectors of the economy, such policies unquestionably benefited other, powerful interests whose ability to influence government long pre-dated fascism and on whose continued acquiescence the regime's survival largely depended: heavy industry, the *agrari* of the Po Valley, and the less enterprising big landowners of other regions. These agrarian interests were the true victors in Mussolini's much-trumpeted 'battle for grain', inaugurated in 1925 to free Italy from the cost of importing grain by turning more land over to wheat.

The onset of the world depression in 1929 forced the fascist regime along new paths. The vulnerability of Italy's banks led the government to intervene more directly in the economy, especially following the creation in 1933 of the Institute for Industrial Reconstruction (IRI), a state holding company for private funds which thereafter increasingly took over from private banks the task of investing in industrial development. The Ethiopian war of 1935–6 gave renewed impetus to what in 1936 became Mussolini's declared policy: that of 'autarky' or economic self-sufficiency, deemed essential for a warrior nation. From 1935 onwards the state's role in industrial financing, raw material allocation, the replacement of imported by home-produced materials, and direct control of major industries increased. By 1939 it controlled over four-fifths of Italy' s shipping and shipbuilding, three-quarters of her pig-iron production and almost half that of steel. This level of state intervention greatly surpassed that in Nazi Germany, giving Italy a public sector second only to that of Stalin's Russia. The difference lay, of course, in the survival in Italy of an increasingly concentrated private sector: for example, two firms, Montecatini and SNIA Viscosa, monopolized the entire chemical industry. Powerful private interests may have mistrusted the state's growing role, not to mention the dangerous purposes towards which Italy's still uneven economic resources were by the late 1930s being directed. They were nevertheless too compromised to extricate themselves from a system that continued to benefit them.

Disputes continue to rage among historians as to the effects of fascist economic policies, and in particular their relationship with the 'modernization' of Italy. The issue of 'modernization' will be explored later; what bare statistics on growth and productivity conceal, however, is the sometimes deliberate and sometimes accidental unevenness with which fascist economic policies, and the social priorities governing them, affected different areas of Italian society. The most obvious beneficiaries have already emerged: cosseted northern industrialists, rural landlords and agrarian capitalists, their products protected and their wage bills held down by fascist labour policies. Between the curbing of inflation in 1925–6 and its return in the late 1930s, substantial elements of the urban upper and lower middle class also had cause for satisfaction. Expanding state and party bureaucracies provided opportunities for employment and status even during the depression; an expanding education system created new posts for would-be teachers and qualifications for a rapidly increasing number of middle-class students; and the disciplining of organized labour provided them with a new sense of status and security. Less fortunate were the middling layers of rural society, those small property-owners, tenant farmers and sharecroppers, many of whom had looked to fascism for improved prospects. Under fascism the numbers of peasant proprietors, which had been increasing since the war, declined again, while rising numbers of tenants and sharecroppers found their terms and conditions deteriorating. Fascist propaganda idealized rural life and advocated 'ruralization' rather than continued urban growth; nevertheless, the realities of rural existence under fascism caused the

35

flight from the land to accelerate. This process, and the flow of population northwards, were intensified by the still widening gap between northern Italy, which under fascism continued to develop and enjoyed relative prosperity, and the south, devastated by policies such as the 'battle for grain' and now deprived of its traditional emigration outlets in the United States and South America.

The effects of fascist policies on the working class were mixed, recent historical research suggesting that they were less harsh, in purely material terms at least, than used to be believed. On the one hand, working-class Italians were no longer defended by their own trade unions, were forbidden to organize in their own interests and, as we have seen, derived little benefit from the machinery of the corporate state. Industrial workers suffered officially imposed wage cuts in 1927, 1930 and 1934, while agricultural labourers' money wages declined during the early 1930s by between 20 and 40 per cent. Nor did dictatorship render Italy as immune from the 1930s slump as the regime's propaganda tried (with considerable success) to suggest. Official figures admitted to the existence of a million unemployed by 1933; the true figure was certainly much higher, with millions more (especially in agriculture) *under*-employed, and working women forced back into the home.

It is nevertheless only proper to recognize, first, that although money wages may have declined dramatically, real wages, thanks to falling prices during the early and mid-1930s, held up better, dropping between 1925 and 1938 by an average of at most 10 per cent (a figure which some authorities would consider too high); second, that the level of unemployment would have been higher had it not been for the regime's investment and public works policies; third, that while the corporate state proper may have done little for workers, the fascist unions, or syndicates, not only continued to function alongside the corporations but also managed to provide their members (whose numbers increased considerably during the 1930s) with some protection and benefits; fourth, that the fascist state increased the provision of social insurance (against unemployment, injury, etc.) available to workers; and finally, that new institutions like the [Dopolavoro] undoubtedly did something to cushion the effects of hardship and slightly to enrich otherwise monotonous working-class lives.

Set up
1925 - one of M's
popular initiatives

The totalitarian dream

According to official theory and propaganda, fascism was a 'totalitarian' system requiring not merely the passive conformity of all Italians but their sincere commitment to, and active participation in, a heroic enterprise of national regeneration. Superficial observers of Italian life during the 1930s believed this goal was being realized. Fascist propaganda was all-pervasive and censorship of alternative views effective. The Mussolini cult with its liturgical slogans – 'Mussolini is always right', 'Believe, Obey, Fight!' – was inescapable. Fascist uniforms, officials and militia were everywhere. Trains – at least on the main lines – ran on time. Malarial marshes – at least near Rome where they could be viewed by visiting foreigners – were drained and cultivated. Even the country's sportsmen obliged with success; in addition to the triumphs of its athletes and cyclists, Italy's footballers won the World Cup twice under fascism, in 1934 and 1938, as well as the Olympic championship in 1936.

In reality, however, the fascist regime fell well short of the totalitarianism claimed by its spokesmen and ascribed to it by some contemporary and later political scientists. The fundamental reason lay in early fascism's need, born of its varied and confused character, to make compromises with powerful established interests in order to achieve power. From 1922 to 1929 Mussolini completed this process. The economic policies pursued after 1925, for example, were in part adopted to placate uneasy industrialists and landowners, whilst in 1929 came Mussolini's greatest coup thus far – the Lateran Accords with the papacy. The agreement, creating the Vatican state and erecting a complete framework for church–state relations within Italy, ended the sixty-year-old feud between the Kingdom of Italy and the papacy; for Mussolini it sealed his alliance with conservative forces and ensured the support of countless Italian Catholics who might otherwise have been half-hearted or hostile towards him.

Autonomous, conservative interests – monarchy, industry, landowners, armed forces and the church – thus formed an integral part of Mussolini's regime, making it less profoundly 'fascist' in its essential character and less totalitarian in scope than it pretended to be. Just as Mussolini remained until 1943 constitutionally subordinate to the King, so despite all efforts to the contrary on the part of militant fascists – and, occasionally, of Mussolini himself – his conservative allies retained considerable autonomy within their particular spheres of operation. To cite merely one example: the church, notwithstanding sometimes bitter disputes with the government, maintained a powerful hold over areas of Italian life vital to a would-be totalitarian regime – education and the private consciences of believers. The effect of this diluting of the regime's supposed totalitarianism, paradoxically, was to enhance Mussolini's personal authority. In return for preserving some autonomy, his conservative allies effectively abandoned any idea of concerted action and surrendered to the Duce an awesome freedom to formulate and implement general, and especially foreign, policy.

Even among the population at large, fascism's impact was uneven. Throughout much of rural, and especially southern, Italy another of fascism's compromises allowed existing power structures to survive, either alongside or actually disguised as those of the party. The village of Gagliano in the southern region of Lucania, immortalized in Carlo Levi's *Christ Stopped at Eboli*, exemplifies fascism's failure to impinge on everyday rural life, save as the latest device for perpetuating the control of the locally dominant. Urban Italians might be exposed to fascist propaganda through school, press, radio, cinema, and the various organizations of the party, but such things barely penetrated the southern countryside. With one southern power-group, however, the fascist regime refused to compromise. In Sicily the Mafia, whose ability to operate its own system of administration and 'justice' was plainly incompatible with 'totalitarianism', was resolutely pursued and apparently suppressed; events were nevertheless to prove its capacity to survive underground.

The hyperactive atmosphere of urban Italy may have suggested otherwise, but Mussolini was in reality obliged to settle for conformity rather than the universal activism necessary to totalitarianism. On this restricted level, at least, the regime during the 1930s recorded considerable success. The coercive capacities of police, OVRA and fascist militia played a major part in this, as did the enervating effects upon potentially troublesome elements of occupational insecurity and the destruction of old political and trade-union networks. Fear of dismissal ensured the quiescence of the rising numbers of public employees, notably the great mass of school-teachers and university professors who in the 1930s swore an oath of loyalty to the regime; out of 1250 professors, only 11 refused. Propaganda, the 'fascistization' of education, and the conditioning effects of youth organizations, the Dopolavoro, etc., if not creating as many passionate fascists as was intended, did help secure acquiescence; if they failed to make popular a party widely and rightly considered corrupt, they nevertheless did make a hero of Mussolini. And it is essential to recognize that for many Italians the regime's achievements, magnified by propaganda, were very real: social peace at home and respect abroad were agreeable novelties to politically conscious Italians previously accustomed to social uncertainty and international humiliation. This widespread if largely passive acceptance of the regime during the early 1930s has inspired a leading Italian historian of fascism, Renzo De Felice, to call these the 'years of consensus'.

For two categories of Italians, passive consensus was anathema. The opposition, composed from the late 1920s of isolated individuals, small clandestine groups and trade-union cells, was courageous but weak, barely succeeding in keeping alive a flicker of resistance which would later grow into something much greater. Many of its leading figures were driven into foreign exile or, like Carlo Levi, punished by internal exile to remote parts of their own country. At the other extreme stood those fascists for whom the regime's accomplishments were insufficient. Resentful of the continued power of the crown, capitalists and church, acutely aware of fascism's failure to bridge the gulf between state and people, and envious of the more extreme course being pursued by Nazism in Germany, radical fascists insistently demanded further advances towards true totalitarianism. In 1938 one such group was rewarded with the adoption of racial laws – this in a country with only 45,000 Jews (some of them hitherto supporters of fascism) and no anti-Semitic tradition. Other fascist malcontents looked for greater progress in a socially radical, neo-syndicalist direction, but remained disappointed. Nothing more graphically illustrates fascism's limitations as a totalitarian regime than the endless yearnings of its own militants for a 'fascist revolution' that never came.

7

Diplomacy and imperialism, 1922–36

Fascism and foreign affairs

Historians still disagree over Mussolini's conduct of foreign affairs in the years between his assumption of the premiership and the conquest of Ethiopia in 1935–6. Some hold the view, once dominant on the left, that the imperialism of the 1930s was the largely unpremeditated response to domestic problems of a dictator whose chief concern was always the internal consolidation of his regime. More recently, however, the balance of opinion has tended to tilt towards a belief in the underlying consistency of Mussolini's foreign policy: a policy, it is argued, always expansionist in intent even when moderately conducted. What has seldom been doubted is Mussolini's controlling hand in the making of policy. For long periods he was his own foreign secretary, and even when he was not – between 1929 and 1932 when Dino Grandi was foreign secretary and after 1936 when the post was held by his own son-in-law Galeazzo Ciano – his essential control persisted. Although initially his conduct of foreign affairs may have been guided and even restrained by foreign office officials and their permanent head, Contarini, such restraints soon disappeared, first as Mussolini simply overrode or bypassed his bureaucrats and then as the foreign office was partially 'fascistized'.

Most countries' foreign policies operate along fairly well-worn paths, and those of post-war Italy were no exception. Her chief areas of interest remained the Mediterranean, Africa and the Balkans, whilst the principal determinant of her international position continued to be her economic and military weakness. The war and the post-war settlement solved one major problem for Italy but, in many Italians' eyes, left others still awaiting solution. The disintegration of Austria-Hungary removed the most serious threat to Italian security, yet both irredentist claims around the Adriatic and imperialist dreams of African and Middle-Eastern empires remained unsatisfied.

As a crucial element in fascism's rise to power, the myth of 'mutilated victory' (see p. 15) was certain to form a central theme of Mussolini's foreign policy. Fascism's original 1919 programme, tinged as it was with socialism and democracy, admittedly gave little sign of what lay ahead; imperialism was repudiated and the intention to pursue Italy's Adriatic claims legally was stressed. All this changed as fascism itself changed. The vast influx of active recruits to fascism between 1920 and 1922 included large numbers of chauvinistic war veterans; D'Annunzio's exploits at Fiume gave fascism, and Mussolini in particular, much to live up to; and after the March on Rome fascism's new ethos was further reinforced by the absorption of Nationalists and other conservatives. The Nationalists' conception of Italy's international role was aptly expressed by Federzoni: 'We Italians like to be loved, but prefer to be envied and feared.' Henceforth all the main fascist factions – ex-Nationalists, ex-syndicalists, technocrats and *squadristi* – advocated a 'revisionist' foreign policy aimed at modifying in Italy's favour a peace settlement deemed insulting to her status as a victor.

There is no reason to believe that Mussolini's views by now differed from these. Among the influences which had obliterated his socialism were at least two favourable not only to a revisionist policy but also to the use of force in pursuing it: the belief in perpetual international struggle held by both Nationalists and many ex-syndicalists, and directed chiefly against 'decadent' France; and the Futurists' exaltation of modern technology, weaponry and war. The resultant cocktail was a dangerously intoxicating one, especially when consumed by someone as vain, capricious, violent and authoritarian in temperament as Mussolini. Whilst it may therefore be misleading to speak of a coherently conceived and consistently pursued revisionist foreign policy or of a 'plan' for imperial conquest, there can be little doubt that revisionism did constitute the prime inspiration for Mussolini's behaviour in the international arena.

This conclusion is reinforced by the essentially militaristic nature of Mussolini's domestic policies, so many of which, significantly, were depicted in terms of 'battle'. Fascism's 'battle for births' aimed, by encouraging large families, to boost Italy's population chiefly in order to provide her armed forces with manpower and justify demands for more territory. The purpose of the 'battle for grain' was to make Italy self-sufficient in the most important of all basic foodstuffs so that this rising population, steeped in militaristic values and quasi-military disciplines by fascist education and fascist propaganda, could be adequately fed in times of war. And fascist industrial policy, as we have seen, sacrificed export industry in favour of the heavy industry necessary to war production. These were not the policies of a regime, or of a leader, likely to settle for lasting peace.

Mussolini's diplomacy, 1922–32

Whatever Mussolini's inclination, during the 1920s the domination of Europe by France and Britain precluded not merely an aggressively revisionist foreign policy but also the kind of international equilibrium necessary for Italy to enjoy diplomatic importance as a potential upsetter of the balance of power. The Duce accordingly restricted himself to mostly verbal defiance of the post-war status quo and to the somewhat contradictory pursuit, which he was never wholly to abandon, of acceptance as a 'respectable' statesman of continental stature, capable of obtaining gains for Italy through skilful diplomacy. He nevertheless remained restless, his open scorn for Anglo-French democracy and League of Nations pacifism sharpened by intense jealousy for French and British power. France's African empire, her diplomatic web in south-eastern Europe, and her harbouring of Italian anti-fascist *émigrés* especially enraged him; British control of Gibraltar, Malta and Suez, and consequent presence in the Mediterranean, were also irksome, though Mussolini's envy of Britain, like Hitler's, was mixed with admiration.

His first year as premier saw Mussolini operating as both

adventurer and diplomatist. A combination of boldness and negotiation enabled him to better D'Annunzio and achieve Fiume's incorporation in Italy; the terms of Mussolini's agreement with Yugoslavia consigned Fiume to isolation from its hinterland and consequent economic stagnation, but Italian patriots, ecstatic at Fiume's 'redemption', preferred to ignore such uncomfortable details. Less successful was Mussolini's impetuous occupation of the Greek island of Corfu, which international and especially British pressure forced him to evacuate. Having learned that he could not yet defy those more powerful than himself, Mussolini for almost a decade trod more warily, seeking to strengthen Italy's position through maintaining good relations with Britain while working to undermine France's alliance system in south-eastern Europe. Crucial to this strategy was his friendly relationship with the British foreign secretary Austen Chamberlain, one of the many European conservatives who admired the Duce's anti-bolshevism and imposition of internal 'order'. Chamberlain's benevolence ensured British acquiescence in the establishment of an Italian protectorate over Albania in 1926 and made possible the cession to Italy of two small pieces of African territory.

Italy's interests in both Africa and the Balkans remained very much alive and were pursued by Mussolini in ways not always entirely 'respectable'. The Albanian protectorate was merely one way of extending Italian influence in south-eastern Europe; others included the encouragement of subversive movements, especially in Yugoslavia, and the signing in 1927 of a treaty with another revisionist state under right-wing rule, Hungary. The goal of such activities was the replacement of French by Italian influence in the Balkans and the fulfilment of Italian claims around the Adriatic, if necessary through the dismemberment of Yugoslavia. In Africa fascist policies between 1922 and 1932 were epitomized by the ruthless subjection of the Arab and Berber population of Libya and the signing in 1928 of a treaty of 'friendship' with Ethiopia. Friendship, as later events were to show, was the last thing on Mussolini's mind.

By the late 1920s Mussolini's impatience with formal diplomacy was rising – in part, perhaps, because of the disrespectful attitude displayed towards his diplomatic posturings by uncensored foreign journalists and cartoonists. His language on international issues was becoming more strident, and from 1928 'revisionism' was official policy. Prudence nevertheless remained necessary in practice. For all Mussolini's rhetoric concerning Italy's supposedly 5-million-strong, swiftly mobilizable army and her airforce capable of 'blotting out the sun', she was still poorly prepared for serious military conflict. The onset of the depression in 1929, forcing cuts in military budgets where Mussolini would have preferred lavish expenditure, dictated another three years of caution. It was this, rather than any underlying shift of policy or the moderation of Grandi as foreign secretary, that inspired the latter's support in this period for disarmament and the League of Nations.

In July 1932 Mussolini resumed the foreign secretaryship and proceeded to fill important foreign office posts with committed fascists. Earlier tactical ambivalence was now largely abandoned, and policies clearly perceptible from the late 1920s were intensified. The Duce had become deeply frustrated at what seemed the sparse achievements of his relative diplomatic propriety. Negotiation over Africa and diplomatic manoeuvring in the Balkans were coming to seem less appealing and glorious than terrorism and imperialism. Other considerations doubtless pushed him in the same direction: at home the PNF had lost its political role and the corporativist experiment was running out of steam, yet fascism's 'revolutionary' appetite still demanded nourishment; relations with the Vatican had stabilized; in Italy's existing colonies resistance had been crushed; and in Europe the era of Anglo-French monopoly was drawing to a close. The Duce, who a decade earlier had assured foreigners that 'fascism is not for export', now increasingly laid claim to an ideological conception of foreign policy: this was to be the era of fascism, in which Italy's imperial destiny would be fulfilled at last.

Ethiopia

Hitler's assumption of the German chancellorship in January 1933 transformed the European scene. How this was eventually to affect Italy was not at first apparent, especially since Mussolini had until quite recently been dismissive of Nazism. Although flattered by the rise to power in Germany of a man who openly venerated him, the Duce could not be entirely comfortable with the new situation. On the one hand the re-entry of a nationalistic Germany to the international stage could be expected to make the British, and still more the French, take Italy more seriously; on the other, Hitler's known designs on Austria threatened to recreate, in far more menacing form, the threat to Italy's north-eastern borders once posed by Austria-Hungary. It was to ward off such a possibility that Mussolini had for some time sponsored the Austrian Heimwehr fascists and in 1934 supported the authoritarian Catholic regime of the Austrian chancellor, Dollfuss. When Austrian Nazis launched an unsuccessful *coup d'état* and assassinated Dollfuss in July 1934, Mussolini moved troops to the Austrian frontier as a warning to Germany. Hitler had no intention of intervening at this stage, but the move boosted Mussolini's standing and morale.

Mussolini's hopes of exploiting the new continental balance in order to become the arbiter of Europe were frustrated during 1933–4 by British and French resistance. The Duce was nevertheless correct in anticipating that Britain and France would allow him greater freedom of action in another area which was increasingly preoccupying him. Plans for the conquest of Ethiopia had long been under way when a convenient incident on the Somaliland–Ethiopia frontier in December 1934 enabled Italy to raise the level of tension. Mussolini, in rejecting mediation, relied on Franco-British amenableness and was richly rewarded. At the Stresa conference of April 1935, involving Italy, France and Britain and convened in response to German 'revisionism', the French and British studiously avoided mentioning Ethiopia; later in the year Britain went so far as to offer Mussolini a slice of Ethiopian territory. Only bloodshed would now satisfy Mussolini, however, and on 3 October 1935 war began. Anglo-French generosity still had one card to play: the Hoare–Laval pact, intended to offer Mussolini enough of Ethiopia to ensure his control over what remained. Outraged public opinion in Britain forced the scheme's withdrawal before Mussolini's response was known. Meanwhile the League of Nations had voted for economic sanctions against Italy. These proved a farce; the vital commodity of oil was not included, the British refrained from closing the Suez canal to Italian shipping, and no sanctions were imposed by nations such as Germany and the United States who were not League members. By May 1936 the war was over, Italy's east African empire was at last a reality, and the fascist regime had reached its pinnacle of success.

The conquest of Ethiopia represented Mussolini's accomplishment of what had been an Italian nationalist dream for half a century. Neither the problems of the depression nor the African interests of certain industrial pressure groups were sufficient to dictate it. Existing colonies were failing to attract the millions of potential emigrants beloved of fascist propaganda, and were proving unrewarding to the few thousand who actually settled there; moreover, their administration, policing and economic infrastructures constituted a considerable drain on the Italian treasury. The acquisition of Ethiopia, as might easily have been predicted, was simply to aggravate this situation. The explanation for the attack on Ethiopia thus lies in fascism and its Duce. The fascist need for excitement, conflict and dramatic success was perfectly personified in Mussolini himself and sanctified by the puerile *machismo* of the Duce cult. Other dictators such as Franco in Spain and Salazar in Portugal constructed personal cults on the appeal of stability and lack of excitement. Neither Mussolini's personality nor the psychology of fascism rendered such a thing conceivable – fatally, in the end, for both.

8

The decline and fall of fascism, 1936–45

The Duce at war, 1936–43

With the conquest of Ethiopia accomplished, Mussolini stood at a diplomatic crossroads. Whatever his methods, he had not yet stepped outside the well-worn paths of Italian foreign policy. Despite British support of sanctions, those ties with Britain which had formed the most consistent element in his diplomacy remained intact. The Duce's horizons were changing, however, and within weeks, with his acquiescent son-in-law Ciano at the foreign ministry, he was launched on a course that was entirely new. In July 1936 right-wing military and civilian rebels rose against the elected government of the Spanish Republic. Anticipating another swift victory and the extension of Italian influence in the western Mediterranean, Mussolini threw Italian resources into the war on the rebel side. It was to be a major investment: 25,000 troops and militia at the peak in 1937 and over 70,000 in all, together with quantities of aircraft, weapons and ammunition that Italy could ill afford to squander. The war, which dragged on until 31 March 1939, exposed and aggravated Italy's military deficiencies, whilst the rebel victory brought her little significant reward. The defeat of Italian fascist forces at the battle of Guadalajara (March 1937) acquired special significance inflicted in part by the Garibaldi battalion of Italian anti-fascist exiles, it provided anti-fascists within Italy with a double reassurance: that

47

the flame of resistance still burned, and that the power of fascism was not insuperable.

Mussolini's Spanish adventure demonstrated conclusively the new ideological and expansionist direction of his foreign policy: the 'decadent' democracies must learn that this was the 'century of fascism'. The new course was wholly of his own choosing, for the democracies themselves, France and Britain, showed little wish to alienate someone whose friendship in the face of a resurgent Germany they were anxious to retain. It was precisely this resurgence, however, epitomized for Mussolini by Hitler's re-militarization of the Rhineland in March 1936, that convinced him his future lay with Germany. The Axis of October 1936, a loose association initiated and named by Mussolini, marked the first step in what was to prove a fateful relationship; the die was cast in 1938 with Mussolini's adoption of a neutral stance over Germany's absorption of Austria. The contrast with his anti-German belligerence in 1934 was striking, and henceforth the relative positions of the two dictators were reversed. Mussolini, bedazzled by German military strength during a visit in September 1937, was becoming indisputably the lesser figure and Italy the junior partner in the new relationship. Subsequent events re-emphasized Italy's subordinate status. At the October 1938 Munich conference, Mussolini, attempting yet again to pose as arbiter of Europe, was visibly a peripheral figure. Germany's diplomatic success at Munich and her eventual destruction of Czechoslovakia early in 1939 stung a jealous Mussolini into a blatant and pathetic act of emulation: the formal annexation in April 1939 of Italy's Albanian 'protectorate'. In May an uneasy Ciano was pushed by his father-in-law into signing with Germany the Pact of Steel, a military alliance drafted according to German wishes and committing the two states to mutual assistance in the event of any, and not merely defensive, hostilities.

This did not mean that Italy was ready for the kind of war into which the German alliance seemed likely to pull her. When the Germans had first suggested a military alliance in May 1938, Mussolini had demurred on the grounds partly that Italian public opinion was unprepared and partly that Italy would be militarily unready for major hostilities before 1942. Now that the pact existed, but with Italian military and economic resources stretched in east Africa and squandered in Spain, he declared that it would be 1943 before his country could play its part. Coming from a dictator whose dream had been to transform his country into a warrior nation, and who had had almost seventeen years in which to make that dream reality, this was hardly an affirmation of success.

It was, nevertheless, a more-or-less honest appraisal of Italy's state of military preparedness, and showed that Mussolini was far from having lost all grip on reality. The events of 1939–43 showed how right he was to be cautious in 1938–9 and how wrong he later was to ignore his own warning voice. On the outbreak of war in September 1939 he requested of Hitler impossible quantities of arms and raw materials as the price of Italy's immediate participation, receiving instead – as he certainly intended – Hitler's acceptance of Italian neutrality. In spring 1940, however, as the Germans swept across north-western Europe, the Duce, embarrassed at cutting so unheroic a figure, decided to enter what now looked like being a short war while some pickings remained. From the outset Italy's war went badly. Minuscule advances into south-eastern France in June 1940 were followed in October by a disastrously unsuccessful invasion of Greece from which Italy was rescued only by German intervention. In north Africa, the principal sphere allotted by Germany to Italian arms, early advances were rolled back by the British during late 1940 and effective command assumed during 1941 by the Germans under General Rommel. Meanwhile, by mid-1941 Italy's recently won east African empire had been overrun by the British. By now, though, Mussolini's commitment to Hitler was total, leading him unnecessarily to send Italian forces to assist in Germany's invasion of Russia and in December 1941 to commit the ultimate and suicidal absurdity of declaring war on the United States. Italy now stood exposed to the allied counter-offensive which began in November 1942 with the Axis collapse at El Alamein and the Anglo-American invasion of French north Africa. Six months later the Axis forces in north Africa were crushed and on 9 July 1943 allied troops, with the connivance of a re-emerging Mafia, landed in Sicily.

The overthrow of Mussolini

In May 1936, with his regime firmly established and Italy's African destiny apparently realized, Mussolini's standing with his fellow Italians stood at its peak. Thereafter it entered a steady decline. The Spanish adventure, never popular and the less so the longer it endured, began the process. More important, however, was Italy's increasing closeness and subservience to Germany. An intrinsically demeaning relationship was for many Italians made worse by the threatening arrival of Germans on the Brenner frontier in 1938. Most Italians were repelled also by the 1938 racial laws, introduced in what looked like slavish imitation of Nazi racism. Among those who found Mussolini's new course distasteful was the King, whose satisfaction at becoming an emperor was largely cancelled out by his distress at Italy's gradually increasing subservience to Germany. Quite apart from his personal dislike of Hitler (which was fully reciprocated), Vittorio Emanuele had every reason to be suspicious of the Fuehrer's influence over the Duce. By the late 1930s the one-time republican Mussolini, envious of Hitler's complete dominance within Germany and irritated by his own constitutional subordination to the crown, was eager to undermine the monarchy's position. The Duce's assumption of command over the armed forces in 1940 further antagonized a monarch who, as the war went on, grew less inclined to accept Mussolini's indispensability.

Another source of pre-war anti-Germanism was the general and legitimate fear of embroilment in major hostilities. In June 1940, nevertheless, Italian public opinion rallied, somewhat reluctantly and with little sign of real enthusiasm, behind the regime. Probably it is not too cynical to suggest that had Italy's war prospered, Mussolini would have reaped new glory and popularity. Instead, the succession of Italian defeats simply laid bare the emptiness of his bellicose bombast and the all-round shortcomings of fascism as a system. As Italian forces struggled, German influence grew, not only in the war zone but also within Italy itself. Loss of territory and heavy Italian casualties in Russia and Africa encouraged both conservative fellow-travellers and elements within fascism itself to seek a way out of the German alliance. Italy's domestic condition strengthened such desires, with acute shortages of food and other essentials and a renewal of major strike activity in March 1943.

At this point Mussolini precipitated the crisis of his own regime. The Duce was now a sick man, plagued by acute gastric troubles which may have been psychosomatic but were no less debilitating for that. No longer an impressive figure, he was losing the respect of many leading fascists; perhaps sensing it, he surrounded himself with toadies and remained undisturbed by the flagrant corruption both of party hacks and of the numerous relatives of his mistress, Clara Petacci. Between February and April 1943 he demoted several of fascism's leading figures, among them Ciano, Bottai and Grandi. The effect was to throw these disgruntled fascists into the arms of anti-Mussolini conspirators, among them other, mainly moderate, fascists, monarchists, liberal politicians, and important figures within the military and police.

The invasion of Sicily brought matters to a head. On 16 July 1943 the fascist dissenters succeeded in persuading Mussolini to summon the first meeting of the Fascist Grand Council since 1939. Before it took place, Mussolini's position slipped further when, at a meeting with Hitler at Feltre in northern Italy on 19 July, he was as usual dominated by the Fuehrer and shrank from telling him, as his military and political advisers had urged, that Italy could not continue fighting.

The meeting of the Fascist Grand Council during the night of 24–25 July saw Mussolini under attack from two sides: the 'moderates' led by Ciano, Grandi and Bottai who wished to break with Germany and realized that this necessitated Mussolini's removal; and pro-Germans like Farinacci who wished to cement the German alliance more solidly and accompany this with a revitalized, 'nazified' party revolution at home. The 'moderates' were in the majority and after much discussion carried a motion, amounting to a vote of no confidence in Mussolini, which called for the King to resume command of the armed forces. Mussolini left, not believing that this 'consultative' body could harm him. The King, however, now seized his opportunity and at an interview later on 25 July informed the Duce of his dismissal. As Mussolini left the royal presence he was courteously arrested.

The Italian Social Republic and the final collapse of fascism

On Mussolini's fall the premiership was assumed by a monarchist general, Badoglio, and the way prepared for Italy's surrender; this came on 8 September 1943, to be followed in October by her declaration of war on her recent ally, Germany. The allies'

51

invasion of the southern Italian mainland in early September was met with Germany's formal occupation of northern and central Italy. For the next eighteen months Italy was the stage for two overlapping wars: that between the advancing allies and the Germans, and a civil war between Italian fascists and the rapidly growing Resistance.

The absence of any popular opposition to Mussolini's overthrow and the swift disintegration of fascist organization throughout liberated Italy were stark testimony to fascism's lack of deep roots in Italian society. So, in a different way, was the experience of the new version of fascism which appeared within German-occupied Italy. The Germans, anxious to use Mussolini in order to tie the population to the Axis, on 12 September 1943 carried out an audacious rescue of the Duce from his mountain prison at Gran Sasso. He was then installed as head of a new fascist regime based in the far north of Italy: the Italian Social Republic, more generally known (due to the location of its propaganda headquarters) as the Republic of Salò.

Superficially the Social Republic represented a reversion to the early fascist social radicalism which had been effectively abandoned in the quest for power. Its ruling personnel consisted mostly of second-rank – and second-rate – figures and hitherto frustrated radical fascists; its programme, defined at the Congress of Verona in November 1943, was rabidly republican – understandably in view of the King's dismissal of Mussolini – and anti-Semitic, and whilst guaranteeing private property rights, envisaged both land reform and the involvement of workers and the state in the running of industry. This radicalism, though taken very seriously by its authors – and by many postwar neo-fascists – was a hollow phenomenon. Many fascists refused to pursue its implementation; industrialists effectively resisted it; workers struck against it; and, crucially, the Germans nullified it. For if in theory the Social Republic embodied a return to fascist 'leftism', in reality it demonstrated nothing more than fascism's utter subjection to Nazi Germany. While fascist enthusiasts talked of worker-participation in industry, the Germans ruthlessly dispatched Italian workers to labour in Germany; while fascist nationalism continued undiminished, Germany flouted the Pact of Steel by annexing Italian territory won from Austria-Hungary in 1918–19; and all the while the Social Republic, created by Germans and radical fascists to keep

Italians loyal, presided over the precise opposite as more and more flocked to the Resistance. And if the Republic's programme showed fascism at its most 'progressive', the regime's deeds showed it at its most vindictive: in its brutal treatment of opposition and its pursuit of Mussolini's 'betrayers' within the party. Of these only one leading figure was caught, tried and shot: Mussolini's son-in-law, Ciano.

Meanwhile, the area nominally governed by the Social Republic was shrinking. By August 1944 the allies were as far north as Florence, and during early 1945 they and the Resistance recaptured northern Italy as Germany itself was invaded from both west and east. With his paper regime in shreds, Mussolini, after an abortive attempt to arrange terms with the Resistance, fled northwards under German protection. Captured by the Resistance, he was shot dead with his mistress on 28 April 1945 and his body brought back to Milan. There, in the birthplace of fascism, the Duce made his final, posthumous public appearance – hanging upside-down in a city-square petrol station, exposed to the scorn and hatred of the populace.

9

Interpreting Italian fascism

During its lifetime Italian fascism aroused intense controversy among politically aware Europeans, especially as it came to be seen as merely the first example of a widespread phenomenon. In present-day Italy controversy continues as neo-fascists venerate Mussolini's memory whilst left-wing Italians remain unwilling to view fascism in any but the blackest terms. Among students of Italian fascism numerous interpretations of this elusive period in Italian history struggle for acceptance. The sections which follow offer some of the most important.

Fascism as a symptom of moral decay

Many Italian liberals who witnessed the emergence of fascism and its rise to power were reluctant to regard it as a deep-rooted or complex movement. The philosopher and historian Benedetto Croce, who lived through the fascist period and, indeed, enjoyed such eminence in Italian intellectual life that he was largely immune from fascist censorship, considered fascism to be symptomatic of a temporary moral decline within Italian liberalism. Since the turn of the century, he argued, the liberal 'sense of freedom' had been debased by materialism, nationalism and a growing admiration for 'heroic' figures. The new masses thrust on to the political stage during these years lacked liberal sensitivities and were easily manipulated by a minority of fascist hooli-

54

gans, while the governing class was temporarily corrupt and incompetent. Fascism was thus an interruption in Italy's achievement of ever greater 'freedom', a short-term moral infection from which Italy, by rededicating herself to the ideal of freedom, could just as quickly recover. Ironically, fascist intellectuals and propagandists agreed with Croce concerning the moral degeneracy of liberalism; where they differed was in seeing liberalism as *intrinsically* flawed, and fascism as a cure rather than a symptom.

That liberalism's shortcomings contributed to fascism's appearance and success is undeniable. That these were as recent as Croce suggested, and the liberal 'sense of freedom' previously so central an element of Italian life, is highly questionable. In short, most historians would now agree that this 'idealist' interpretation of fascism leaves much unexplained.

Fascism as a product of 'mass society'

A common approach to the understanding of fascism has been that which stresses the role of supposedly 'amorphous' masses. Rapid industrialization, urbanization, war and demobilization, it is suggested, tore millions of Italians from their traditional roots and destroyed their customary local, personal, socioeconomic and cultural relationships. Powerless and directionless, these abandoned souls fell prey to skilful demagogues and well-organized minorities who were able to use them to challenge the dominance of ruling élites. This view of fascism, like Croce's, was in part shared by many fascists, eager to decry the 'old' regime and to stress fascism's mass appeal whilst denying its connection with any particular social class or classes. In fascist eyes, fascism restored a sense of identity and community to countless individuals alienated from each other by rapid socioeconomic changes.

A related approach to that of 'mass society' theorists was adopted during the interwar period by psychologists such as Erich Fromm and Wilhelm Reich, who employed their respective versions of psychoanalytical theory to explain the susceptibility of individuals and masses to the appeal of fascism. It hardly needs to be said that this categorization of fascism as, in effect, a kind of psychopathological disorder, was decidedly *not* congenial to actual fascists. More recently, a similar brand of analysis had been followed by a school of 'psycho-historians'.

Clearly fascism's rise *was* related to the kinds of changes referred to above, and to the failure of existing political parties to embrace and represent the new forces created by them. Clearly, too, an understanding of the psychological forces driving fascists – whether leaders, activists or mere followers – is valuable if and when we can reliably acquire it. What remain unconvincing in most 'mass society' approaches to fascism – which tend in any case to be unduly influenced by the case of Germany – are the notions, first, that the new masses were predominantly 'amorphous', irrational and merely manipulated, and, second, that fascism can somehow be conveniently diagnosed as a mass psychological disorder. Accumulating historical evidence suggests that at least in the Italian case the great majority of those who, at one level or another, embraced fascism did so as the result of reasoned – which is not of course to say correct – assessment of their interests and often a strong sense of class or group identification.

Fascism as the agent of capitalism

During the 1920s and 1930s European Marxists, especially those who followed the leadership of Moscow, produced a succession of analyses of fascism, all of which argued that fascism was in origin the creation of powerful capitalist interests and that when in power it was essentially their tool. Italian capitalism, they insisted, was by the early 1920s incapable of further expansion and therefore created fascism in order to repress the working class and impose a static, protected economy on Italy.

It is certainly true that a close relationship existed between the fascist regime and both industrial and agricultural capitalists, and indeed that the regime would probably not have been born without their assistance. The interwar orthodox Marxist account was nevertheless misleading in several respects – as perceptive Italian communists such as Antonio Gramsci and Palmiro Togliatti recognized. First, it ignored the importance of fascism's mass following and its emergence independently of capitalist interests; second, it failed adequately to explain why in this particular context such interests preferred an alliance with fascism to continued acceptance of a liberalism itself highly favourable to capitalism; third, it exaggerated the importance of such interests in the formulation of policy within the fascist state; and fourth, its depiction of a static or contracting economy under fascism was simply inaccurate.

Fascism as a variety of 'totalitarianism'

A once popular approach to fascism, now perhaps beginning to recover some ground after a quarter of a century in the intellectual wilderness, holds it to be merely one version of a much broader phenomenon, that of 'totalitarianism'. Here the stress is on the fascist regime rather than the movement or the context out of which it emerged. Stressing such features as the role of the leader, the single party, the official monopoly of repressive power and of the mass media, and the directed economy, the proponents of this thesis conclude that the similarities between supposedly different kinds of totalitarian regime greatly outweigh the differences.

The heyday of the 'totalitarianism' thesis was the early part of the Cold War. During the late 1940s and the 1950s it was employed by (mainly American) political scientists to highlight the resemblances between the West's new enemy, the Soviet Union, and the old enemy, fascism. In its favour is the undeniable fact that for most of the population life under one form of 'totalitarian' regime may be much like life under another; under both fascism and communism, fundamental liberal freedoms – of speech, writing and publication, of movement and assembly, of political and trade-union activity, etc. – disappear, while the fruits of economic effort and the exercise of power over others are enjoyed disproportionately by minorities: wealthy capitalists and members of the party hierarchy under fascism and the latter alone under communism. The 'totalitarianism' approach was largely discredited from the 1960s onwards, as historians took over the study of fascism from political scientists. Their dissection of fascist *movements* as well as of detailed aspects of fascist *regimes* tended to bring out the differences, rather than any similarities, between fascism and communism; in the Italian case in particular, historical research exposed how far the goal of totalitarianism was from actually being accomplished.

The differences between communist and fascist *regimes* and even more between the *ideas, movements and circumstances* out of which they respectively emerged, remain evident and

57

important. It is nevertheless possible that a new version of the 'totalitarian thesis' may gain currency following the collapse of Soviet and Eastern European communism during the late 1980s. The manner of this collapse, suggesting that communist regimes were not, after all, 'more totalitarian' than fascist ones, together with such striking subsequent developments as the propensity of ex-communists to embrace a fascist-style, sometimes racially inspired, authoritarian nationalism, are likely to redraw scholarly attention towards those areas where fascism and communism might be said to have had features in common.

Fascism as an agent of 'modernization'

In recent years many students of Italian fascism, including both a non-Marxist majority and a Marxist minority, have come to view fascism as related to Italy's economic backwardness and to attempts at its 'modernization'. Comparisons have been made with other dictatorships seeking rapid industrialization – for example, Stalin's Russia – which have also controlled labour, held down wages and directed investment into heavy industry. Although some economic historians believe that in Italy's case the attempt failed, owing to Mussolini's deference to 'traditional' economic interests, the majority consider that fascism *did* play an important part in 'modernizing' an economy which, for all the development since 1900, was still backward after the 1914–18 war.

This approach appears to be vindicated by generalized economic statistics dealing with overall production and investment, by the development of 'modern' industrial and agricultural sectors under fascism, and by the 'productivist' thread running through the regime. Its critics have warned, however, against mistaking fascism's often improvised economic policies for purposefulness; against ignoring both the extent and the character of pre-fascist industrial development, both of which influenced the shape it assumed under fascism; and against taking at face value the impressive apparatus of state intervention when private interests continued to benefit from the activities of the IRI and the Corporate State. Whether Italy would have modernized more or less without fascism we can never know; whether fascism itself was responsible for such modernization as did occur is problematical; and in any case to

58

view fascism solely in these terms is to pay insuffficient attention to both the manner of its emergence and the human cost of its two decades in power.

Fascism as the revolution of a rising middle class

Since the early 1960s the Italian historian Renzo De Felice has been producing, among other works on fascism, a monumental, multi-volume biography of Mussolini. In the process he has presented an interpretation of fascism which has aroused great controversy, especially within Italy itself, where fascism is a matter not of distant history but of personal recollection and surviving passions. De Felice has argued that the fascist *movement* was primarily one of an 'emerging middle class' eager to challenge the traditional, liberal political class for power. The spirit of this new middle class, he asserts, was 'vital', 'optimistic' and creative; its ideologies were the rational ones of productivism and corporativism; it was, in short, a 'revolutionary phenomenon'. De Felice nevertheless recognizes the compromises made by Mussolini in order to win power, and that the resultant fascist regime was in many respects a 'conservative regime' against which what he terms 'fascism as movement' – the revolutionary impulse within fascism – struggled, largely in vain, until the very end. A fascist regime was not, according to De Felice, inevitable. Mussolini's conservative allies could have prevented fascism's accession to power and, indeed, have re-invigorated liberalism, but chose not to do so. None the less, he concludes, a 'totalitarian' threat to these conservative interests persisted and, had the war not put an end to fascism, might well have been stepped up.

De Felice's conclusions concerning the role of an 'emergent middle class' have, on the whole, been more widely accepted by other historians than his views on the fascist movement's air of optimism and creativity; these, his critics assert, lead him to pay insufficient attention to the negative and brutal side of fascism, which was at least as prominent.

Conclusion

As the volume of serious historical literature on the different aspects of Italian fascism increases, and as the passage of time makes possible clearer perspective and greater objectivity, it becomes evident how complex a phenomenon it was. The underlying conditions – which did not, of course, constitute a *cause* – arose from the failure of Italian liberals, during and immediately after the Risorgimento, to involve more of the population in the nation's affairs. Even as the years passed, the country's leaders were slow to move resolutely towards a broader-based political system. When greater democracy did arrive, it did so with explosive suddenness – between 1912 and 1922, when Italy was faced with the convulsive effects of war, post-war economic crises, mass demobilization, frustrated nationalism and acute social unrest. Such problems, of which social unrest was probably the most important, might have been more easily absorbed by an already established parliamentary system. It was liberal Italy's misfortune to confront acute social conflict *and* the arrival of the 'masses' on the political stage at the same time. Worse still, in post-war 'democratic' Italy, hundreds of thousands, perhaps millions, of Italians had no habitual or obvious political allegiance. Among them were two large and overlapping groups: war veterans, unrewarded for their sacrifices and belittled by the left; and assorted middle-class elements, some conforming to De Felice's picture of a rising and ambitious class, others, especially in the countryside, more closely resembling the fearful, declining *petite bourgeoisie* of Marxist accounts. These Italians, attached neither to traditional liberalism, nor to political Catholicism, nor yet to socialism, comprised fascism's mass base.

Fascism obtained power not through revolution but as the result of Mussolini's compromise with conservative and ostensibly liberal interests. Many of fascism's activists achieved office, status and a measure of power within the regime which subsequently emerged, but the *total* revolution of which some dreamed never materialized. Instead, the regime evolved into one strongly fascist in external appearances, limited in its supposed totalitarianism by the survival of autonomous, mainly conservative forces, and distinguished by the personal power of its Duce. If Mussolini's regime may be said to have served the interests of his conservative allies in certain respects, this was neither deliberately and consistently intended nor necessarily bound to prove permanent. By the 1930s the decisions most liable to affect Italy's future lay in the realm of foreign policy and rested not in the hands of capitalists or militant fascists but in those of Mussolini himself. It was those decisions, taken independently and increasingly against the wishes of his conservative fellow-travellers, that led to Mussolini's downfall and the collapse of fascism.

Suggested reading

Books available in paperback (as of late 1993) are marked*; place of publication is London unless otherwise stated.

The two most satisfactory general textbooks on modern Italian history are Martin Clark, *Modern Italy 1871–1982* (Longman, 1984)* and Denis Mack Smith, *Italy: A Modern History* (Ann Arbor, Mich., University of Michigan Press, 2nd edn 1969).

The most up-to-date general treatment of Italian fascism is Alexander De Grand, *Italian Fascism* (Lincoln, Nebr., University of Nebraska Press, 2nd edn 1989)*; a satisfactory alternative is Alan Cassels, *Fascist Italy* (Arlington Heights, Ill., Harlan Davidson Inc., 2nd edn 1985). Brief overviews are provided by S. J. Woolf, 'Italy', in S. J. Woolf (ed.), *Fascism in Europe* (Methuen, 1981), 39–64; Adrian Lyttelton, 'Italian fascism', in Walter Laqueur (ed.), *Fascism. A Reader's Guide* (Wildwood House, 1976), 125–50; and Roland Sarti, 'Italian fascism: radical politics and conservative goals', in Martin Blinkhorn (ed.), *Fascists and Conservatives* (Unwin Hyman, 1990)*, 14–30. David Forgacs (ed.), *Rethinking Italian Fascism* (Lawrence & Wishart, 1986)*, is an interesting collection of essays on a variety of themes.

Fascism's foundation and rise to power, and the early stages of the fascist dictatorship, are studied in Adrian Lyttelton, *The Seizure of Power. Fascism in Italy, 1919–29* (Weidenfeld &

Nicolson, 1973; 2nd edn, Princeton, N.J., Princeton University Press, 1989*); A. Rossi (a.k.a. A. Tasca), *The Rise of Italian Fascism* (New York, Gordon Press, 1976), offers a contemporary view from the left. Several regional studies provide a sharp focus on this period: Donald Bell, *Sesto San Giovanni. Workers, Culture and Politics in an Italian Town, 1880–1922* (New Brunswick, N.J., Rutgers University Press, 1986); Anthony L. Cardoza, *Agrarian Elites and Italian Fascism. The Province of Bologna 1901–1926* (Princeton, N.J., Princeton University Press, 1982); Paul Corner, *Fascism in Ferrara* (Oxford, Oxford University Press, 1974); Alice Kelikian, *Town and Country under Fascism. The Transformation of Brescia, 1915–26* (Oxford, Clarendon Press, 1986); Frank Snowden, *Violence and Great Estates in the South of Italy* (Cambridge, Cambridge University Press, 1986) and, by the same author, *The Fascist Revolution in Tuscany, 1919–22* (Cambridge, Cambridge University Press, 1989).

A wide-ranging exploration of Italian life under fascism can be found in Edward R. Tannenbaum, *Fascism in Italy. Society and Culture, 1922–45* (Allen Lane, 1972); particular aspects are covered in Victoria De Grazia, *The Culture of Consent. Mass Organization of Leisure in Fascist Italy* (Cambridge, Cambridge University Press, 1981) and, by the same author, *How Fascism Ruled Women. Italy 1922–1945* (Berkeley, Calif., University of California Press, 1992); Christopher Duggan, *Fascism and the Mafia* (New Haven, Conn., Yale University Press, 1989); Tracy Koon, *Believe, Obey, Fight. Political Socialization of Youth in Fascist Italy 1922–1943* (Chapel Hill, N.C., University of North Carolina Press, 1985); and Luisa Passerini, *Fascism in Popular Memory. The Cultural Experience of the Turin Working Class* (Cambridge, Cambridge University Press, 1987).

Fascism's relationship with big business is analysed in Roland Sarti, *Fascism and the Industrial Leadership in Italy* (Berkeley, Calif., University of California Press, 1971), and that with the Vatican in John Pollard, *The Vatican and Italian Fascism, 1929–32* (Cambridge, Cambridge University Press, 1985).

Three books deal with important strands within fascism. The Nationalist right is examined in Alexander De Grand, *The Italian Nationalist Association and the Rise of Fascism in Italy* (Lincoln, Nebr., University of Nebraska Press, 1978), and the syndicalist 'left' in David D. Roberts, *The Syndicalist Tradition and Italian Fascism* (Manchester, Manchester University Press, 1979). The Fascist intelligentsia is covered in Michael Ledeen, *Universal Fascism* (New York, Howard Fertig Inc., 1972).

On foreign policy, imperialism and war see Denis Mack Smith, *Mussolini's Roman Empire* (Harmondsworth, Penguin, 1976); Esmonde M. Robertson, *Mussolini as Empire-Builder. Europe and Africa, 1932–36* (Macmillan, 1977); and MacGregor Knox, *Mussolini Unleashed. Politics and Strategy in Fascist Italy's Last War* (Cambridge, Cambridge University Press, 1982)*.

The most recent serious biography of Mussolini in English is Denis Mack Smith, *Mussolini* (Granada, 1983); also still available is Christopher Hibbert, *Mussolini* (Harmondsworth, Penguin, 1986)*. Although Renzo De Felice's multi-volume biography has not appeared in English, his interpretation is available in his *Fascism. An Informal Introduction to its Theory and Practice* (New Brunswick, N.J., Transaction Books, 1977). Another controversial interpretation of fascism is that of A. James Gregor, *Italian Fascism and Developmental Dictatorship* (Princeton, N.J., Princeton University Press, 1979).

A number of other Lancaster Pamphlets contain material relevant to that discussed here. Important background is provided by John Gooch, *The Unification of Italy*. Italy's African interests are placed within a wider international setting in J. M. MacKenzie, *The Partition of Africa*. The general international context of Mussolini's diplomacy is presented in two pamphlets by Ruth Henig, *Versailles and After: Europe 1919–1933* and *The Origins of the Second World War*, while Mussolini's intervention in Spain is discussed in Martin Blinkhorn, *Democracy and Civil War in Spain 1931–1939*. Finally, Mussolini's fellow fascist dictator is covered in Dick Geary, *Hitler and Nazism*.